Hanna
and Walter

Hanna and Walter

A Love Story

Hanna and Walter Kohner
with Frederick Kohner

Random House   New York

Copyright © 1984 by Hanna and Walter Kohner
All rights reserved under International and Pan-American
Copyright Conventions. Published in the United States by
Random House, Inc., New York, and simultaneously in Canada by
Random House of Canada Limited, Toronto.

Library of Congress Cataloging in Publication Data
Kohner, Hanna.
Hanna and Walter.
1. Holocaust, Jewish (1939-1945)—Personal narratives.
2. Kohner, Hanna. 3. Kohner, Walter. 4. Theatrical
agents—California—Los Angeles—Biography. I. Kohner,
Walter. II. Kohner, Frederick. III. Title.
D810.J4K64 1984   940.53'15'03924   83-42750
ISBN 0-394-52164-1

Manufactured in the United States of America
24689753
First Edition

For
Our daughter Julie
and
To the memory of her grandparents
whom she never knew

Acknowledgments

We are grateful to Gary Mehlman, who encouraged us to write this book

—to Maureen and Eric Lasher, who believed in it
—to Samuel A. Brown, who helped in research

We are especially indebted to Robert Cowley, our dedicated editor and friend, whose contributions to this book were invaluable.

Hanna
and Walter

Walter

One morning in January 1935 the white-and-blue flag bearing the crest of the Clary-Aldringens was hoisted on the flagpole of the castle square. It was a great moment. The skating season had started.

The Clary-Aldringens were a feudal Bohemian family, nobility going back to the fifteenth century. Count Clary, as he was known during the Austro-Hungarian monarchy, had had to relinquish his title after the Great War—just like all other aristocrats—and with the birth of the Republic of Czechoslovakia became Herr von Clary-Aldringen. A sprawling park surrounded his castle, and following an old tradition, he opened the skating season. There were two lakes on the magnificent estate of the Clary-Aldringens, the upper lake and the lower one. Having been tested for solidity, the frozen surface of the lower lake was declared safe.

I was twenty years old and I was now living in Prague, a young man, romantic, ambitious, yet unsure of my place in the world. I was one of three sons. My father was a man of considerable charm, wit and unusual enterprise. He was known as the "Kino Kohner." In Teplitz-Schönau, people with the same surname were identified by their profession. One man named Pick, who distributed wine, was called "Wine

Pick." Another, who ran a small noodle factory, was the "Noodle Pick," and a third, an ear, nose and throat specialist, was called the "Nose Pick." There was a "Milk Steiner" and a "Typewriter Steiner." Hence, quite naturally, our father, who managed the first movie house (*Kino*) in town, was called "Kino Kohner." Through my father's connection with the motion picture industry, he was able to get me a job with the Barrandov film studios in Prague.

I had dropped out of the *Gymnasium*—a secondary school for students preparing to enter a university. I left after the fourth year because my grades were disastrously low. But most of all because I was fascinated by show business. I had come home the day of the flag hoisting to spend the weekend with my family. Shortly after my arrival Herbert, my best friend, called me to go skating with him.

It was a fine day, the air clear and crisp, the sky blue. The pond was crowded: children raced, jumped, bounced, fell, bounced up again, flew through the air. Boys and girls chased one another, middle-aged couples moved elegantly along the edges holding hands crosswise. A small orchestra played on the tiny island in the middle of the lake.

At one point Herbert caught up with me. "Let's do the snake!" he yelled—and grabbed my hand.

Intertwining my left hand with Herbert's, I looked around for a link with my right hand. I grabbed a girl passing by. I felt her hand clawing at mine through her gloves. We were now three, but in a minute we were a dozen. The snake got longer, until it stretched from one edge of the lake to the other. We executed quite a few fanciful patterns, helped by the sound of a polka. Suddenly someone pushed me. I let go of Herbert's hand and crashed to the ice. For a moment I was blinded. I had lost my glasses.

The girl on my right had landed on the ice next to me, but she still held on to my hand. I got up and helped her to her feet. We stood there for a moment. I still couldn't focus my eyes. "I've lost my glasses," I told her.

"If you let go of my hand, I'll look for them," she said, laughing.

I released her hand and she found my glasses and put them on my nose. But they were fogged up and I still couldn't see a thing. The girl said that she would clean them. I handed her my glasses and she wiped them with her scarf, and when I had them on again, I saw her for the first time. She had shiny black eyes and a fine-boned, flowering face. Fourteen, I figured. A child.

I invited her for a hot chocolate and we scampered over to the hut. It was cozy there and smelled of chocolate and burned chestnuts, warmth and winter. I bought her some chestnuts and a cup of hot chocolate.

"Aren't you Walter Kohner?"

I nodded—flattered that she knew my name. She told me that she had seen me frequently on the local *corso*, which was situated in the center of town. Under the shade of chestnut trees young and older people met at all seasons, usually between five and six in the afternoon. They came there to look and be looked at, to discuss the town's latest gossip and—above all—to engage in conspicuous flirtation.

A tall, scrawny girl came over, reminding her that

it was getting dark. "You promised your mother, Hanna!"

"Oh God—" she moaned, "I promised I'd be home before five."

I helped her take off her skates. She carried them on the obligatory leather strap.

It wasn't dark yet, but just as we stepped outside, the lights overhead went on, spreading softness over the icy surface. It made every girl look ravishing. Even a child like her.

"*Auf Wiedersehen*," she said.

I watched her grab her girlfriend's hand and disappear into the throng.

All I knew was her first name.

Hanna.

The famous spa of Teplitz-Schönau lies in Czechoslavakia at the foot of the Ore Mountains close to the German border. The region, known as the Sudetenland was inhabited by a German-speaking population, which had lived there for centuries. The Sudetenland had always been a part of Bohemia, which in turn belonged to the Austro-Hungarian Empire. After the end of World War I in 1918 and the Peace Treaty of Versailles, when Czechoslovakia was created, the Sudetenland became a part of Czechoslovakia.

It wasn't only the healing springs that drew people to Teplitz-Schönau. Poets, painters and composers were attracted by the spa. Goethe took up residence year after year, praising the town's rejuvenating powers, Richard Wagner composed part of his *Tannhäuser* here, and a short distance from my parents' home stood the Baroque structure where Beethoven composed his Eighth Symphony.

Toward the end of the nineteenth century the healing springs caved in and muddied waters were pumped to the surface. For a time the town fathers tried to hush up this catastrophe, but the truth, like the bad water, seeped out; all the celebrities and crowned heads who had flocked to Teplitz-Schönau turned to nearby Karlsbad and Marienbad. But even in its declining years, Teplitz-Schönau served as an inspiration of sorts. Ibsen used the incident of the cave-in and the frightened burghers for his play *An Enemy of the People*.

Still, even with its slightly tarnished glory, our town remained a bastion of *Kultur*, boasting excellent schools, a first-class legitimate theater, an opera house, a symphony orchestra and a magnificent library, which compared favorably with that of Prague's world-famous Charles University.

The population of thirty thousand represented a fair cross section of racial and religious groups: predominantly Germans, Czechs, Catholics, Protestants, Jews. They all lived together harmoniously in the Republic of Czechoslovakia under its revered president, Tomáš G. Masaryk.

I loved the town where I was born, felt secure in its surroundings, and cherished my family and friends.

The next time I saw Hanna was a few months later. It was spring and I had come home to spend the summer with my family. The minute I arrived I called Herbert. He suggested that we meet at five at the corso. Soon we were promenading up and down, watching the new crop of girls in their spring dresses. "Tonight is the school dance," Herbert said. "Want to come along?"

I replied that I was not invited.

"You are invited by me," he said importantly— and told me that he was a member of the dance committee and that there was a scarcity of boys anyhow.

The dance was held at the Neptune, a mournful building with the paint flaking off the walls. The Neptune hadn't served as a hotel for quite some time. It was the only place in town with a large auditorium, a hall that had seen an unending string of political conventions, conferences—and once the famous Czech Kludsky circus had used it for its lions, elephants and high-wire act after the big tent had collapsed during a snowstorm.

That night I joined Herbert, who wore a rented tuxedo and looked rather dapper. The auditorium had cleverly been converted into a ballroom. There were flowers and balloons and wall decorations. At the entrance to the hall stood Herr Reichert, the dance teacher of our town, a slender, elegant man with a pleasant face and the manners of a ballet master.

The ballroom was crowded with young, festively dressed people. Most of the boys wore tuxedos; the girls, long evening dresses. Waiters rushed back and forth, balancing trays full of beer and lemonade. It was *de rigueur* that every girl under eighteen had to be accompanied by either a parent or an older sister or brother. The chaperones sat at small tables grouped around the dance floor, ordering refreshments and keeping an eye on their young charges. A small dance band provided the music.

I knew many of the girls who sat along the wall waiting to be asked for a dance. They fidgeted with their dance cards, filled with names of boys who, long before that evening, had reserved their dances. That was when I saw Hanna for the second time. She wore a black velvet dress and high-heeled shoes, and the neckline of her dress was—as we called it then—risqué. She smiled and I went up to her.

"May I have this dance?"

"You may," she said, looking at me happily.

At first we danced silently. "I had hoped you'd be here," Hanna said after a while.

"I'm glad to see you too," I said. "I have thought about you many times. You are Hanna—who?"

"Hanna Bloch."

"Any relation to Friedl?"

"He's my brother," Hanna said. "Tonight he's also my chaperon."

Friedl Bloch was my age. We knew each other the way boys do in a small town, but we had never been friends.

Hanna seemed to know a lot about me. What I had been doing. Why I had dropped out of school. That I was working in Prague at a film studio. She wanted to know what I was really doing there. Would I some-day be a photographer, a director or—possibly—an actor?

"Of course," I said, "an actor."

"How wonderful!" she cried. "You would be great. Maybe you'll be a star one day." We both laughed.

I told her that I would be going to Vienna in the

fall. I hoped to be accepted at the Reinhardt Seminar, the most famous academy in Europe for aspiring actors.

The music stopped; the dance had ended. "A tango, ladies and gentlemen," Herr Reichert announced.

I had hoped to go on dancing with Hanna, but she pointed ruefully at her dance card. She was fully booked—except for the last dance, which traditionally was a waltz.

I entered my name on the one empty spot of her card. Hanna suggested that I join her brother Friedl, who was all alone.

The lights dimmed and the music started. I walked over to Hanna's brother—deciding not to dance with anyone else the rest of the evening.

Friedl and I had a lemonade and talked about our aspirations. He, like my friend Herbert, was a medical student in Prague.

Hanna and her partner came dancing close by and she smiled radiantly and promisingly, and I felt an almost painful twinge of jealousy.

Now, that's silly, I told myself. I had no claim on her, and after all—she was just a child. How old was she anyhow? I asked Friedl and his answer confirmed that I had guessed about right; she was fifteen.

"She certainly looks older," I said.

During the intermission Hanna joined us. She wanted to know why I hadn't danced with another girl. When I told her that I was waiting for her, she blushed.

I rushed over to her as soon as the final waltz was announced. Her partner made his farewell bow. "I'll be waiting for you at the exit," he called after her.

Unreasonably, I was stung. "I had hoped I could accompany you."

"You had—?" she cried.

"Didn't you know—?"

"Wait a moment." She laid her hand against my cheek and ran after the boy. I watched her talk to him, and was even a little pleased when he seemed to grow angry.

On the way home we held hands. I asked her whether I could see her again, and when. As soon as possible. How about in the morning? She had a tennis lesson, but that would be early.

I went to the tennis court, situated in one of the town's lush parks, and watched her. The tennis instructor was a young man by the name of Fritz Urban. He played a murderous game and was the dream of any young girl who came within the perimeter of the two courts. Hanna waved to me when she saw me and I settled down on one of the benches to watch her play. That morning she wore white shorts and a blue sweater; I admired her agility and her lovely legs. Urban fed her some nasty balls, forcing her to chase from one corner of the court to the other, and—possibly impelled by my presence—she got most of her serves and volleyed back with bravura.

She looked pink under the sun when we walked over to the corso after the lesson. It was Sunday morning. From the terrace of the coffeehouse came the strains of the orchestra playing popular waltzes.

We walked up and down the corso a couple of times, young and happy with the world. Because we were quite obviously a "new pair," we received close scrutiny. Hanna swung her racket jauntily, and I waved at my friends. I had made a new conquest and enjoyed the attention.

Finally I took her home, but made a date right away for the late afternoon—in the usually deserted colonnades behind my father's theater. The colonnades were a medieval archway, and it was one of the few places where one could count on privacy—most of the time.

Hanna was ten minutes late and I was ten minutes early. Breathless, she made excuses, but I cut her off, put my arms around her, and pressing her against the dark walls, I kissed her.

"You will not believe it," she said, "but I have never kissed a boy before."

We kissed again. There was a noise. We quickly drew apart. Another couple came along. I didn't know either of them, but the boy and I exchanged conspiratorial glances.

Silently we walked out of the colonnades. Hanna leaned her head against me, and we sauntered through the park.

From then on we met every day, always at different places—the Königshöhe (one of the wooded ridges surrounding the town), the Schlossberg (the ruins of a medieval castle), behind doorways of age-encrusted houses. We sat together on the terrace of the coffeehouse, and at concerts. One evening I even managed to smuggle Hanna into the movie house, where *Ecstasy*, a film strictly forbidden to adolescents because it showed Hedy Lamarr swimming and frolicking nude in the woods, was having a successful run.

My father, however, discovered us. He had a

mercurial temper and one never knew what to expect. This evening, luckily, his mood was genial. "Do I know the young lady?" he asked.

"This is Hanna Bloch," I said nervously.

"Over sixteen, I would guess."

"Almost," Hanna said.

"Hm."

He paused there for a moment, as if deliberating whether or not to pursue the matter further. He patted Hanna on the cheek, at the same time switching on the flashlight he always held in his left hand. "Cute," he said and grinned. "My son has good taste." He left us where he had found us—in the back of one of the few curtained loges.

Dear Papa—how I feared him and how I worshiped him. At the age of thirteen he had had to leave his overcrowded home—he was one of twelve children —and make his own living, starting as a clerk in a men's wear shop in a provincial town. By eighteen he had taught himself to speak three languages, had learned shorthand and typing, and could recite pages of Goethe's *Faust*. I don't know where it started, this desperate struggle to elevate himself from the abject poverty into which he was born. His own father—my grandfather Nathan—had been a sergeant in the Austro-Hungarian army, a tall, defiant-looking man who had to feed his ever-growing family on his niggardly soldier's pension. He died young.

Julius, my father, was the only one of his family who had higher aims in life. He started to travel, to sell. Like Willy Loman in Arthur Miller's play, he became

a man with a shine and a smile—and he sold whatever he thought was salable. There is a faded photo
showing him on a camel's back somewhere in Africa,
complete with lance and burnoose. Another one
was of the first Zionist Congress in Basel, which
my father attended as a reporter for Vienna's *Neue
Freie Presse*.

He was in Geneva on that fateful morning in
September 1908 when Austria's Empress Elizabeth
was stabbed to death on the Quai de Mont Blanc by
the Italian anarchist Luccheni. When he heard the
news, he ran to the nearest post office and sent the
telegram describing the assassination to the *Presse*.

After the end of World War I he founded Czechoslovakia's first film trade paper, the *Filmschau* (later
known as the *Internationale Filmschau*), and acquired
the movie theater in Teplitz-Schönau. My father's
fascination with show business also launched my two
older brothers on their careers. Paul, the oldest, went
to America in 1921 and was already firmly established as a producer (and later as an agent) in Hollywood; Fritz wrote screenplays in London. And now
there was me—whose ambition was to become an
actor.

I had hoped for my father's approval. I was certain
I would get it. After all, I wanted to go into show
business—my father's world. But when I mustered
enough courage to confront him with my plan, he
exploded. "An actor? Never!"

I felt sick to my stomach. A "no" from my father
was a "no." A "never" was worse.

"But why not?"

Didn't he, through his connections, secure the job for me in Prague? I reminded him that I had acted in school performances, had arranged cabaret evenings and once had even played the lead in a popular comedy.

It didn't help. Yes, if I would first learn an honorable profession, that would be different. Wasn't acting an honorable profession? I repeated stubbornly. "And what about Paul and Fritz—?"

"That's different."

I couldn't see the difference, but my father saw it. "Have your brothers put that bug into your ears?"

I protested—of course not! I had never talked to them of my ambition. I was smart enough to understand that I could not aspire to become an actor in Hollywood—after all, my mother tongue was German—but there were dozens and dozens of small city-subsidized theaters, like the one in my hometown, which were always on the lookout for *Nachwuchs*— new blood. If I was accepted by the Max Reinhardt Seminar in Vienna and went through the two-year training course, I would have no difficulty finding an engagement in the provinces. Max Reinhardt, after all, was one of the world's most distinguished and innovative stage directors, and a world-famous teacher.

My mother, who must have been listening, entered the room. Though she rarely dared oppose my father's decision, she now spoke up. She thought I had genuine talent. She virtually begged him to let me go to Vienna and apply for an audition.

My father was astonished. He looked from my mother to me: had we hatched a plot to undermine his parental authority? "First he has to learn a profession," he insisted.

There was a protracted silence.

Then my mother said, "But, Julius—acting *is* a profession."

And so I went to Vienna.

Hanna

I don't think there was ever a time when I wasn't in love.

I was in love with my uncle Sigmund—and I didn't mind his bristly mustache when he kissed me. I was wildly in love with a girl in the first class of the *Gymnasium* who was all I wasn't: tall and pale and blond. I had a crush on every one of my brother's friends who came to the house to do homework. All I ever dared was a shy, soulful look. I was still a child and in love with dreams. At thirteen I started to read romantic novels. I don't remember whether I understood *Anna Karenina*, but I adored Vronsky. My next undying love was Johannes in Knut Hamsun's *Victoria*, and I shed tears for Heathcliff and Gösta Berling.

At fourteen the passionate crushes began: there was Heinrich Percy, a baritone whom I saw for the first time singing Schubert in *Blossom Time*. I wrote on a soft-blue notepaper: "Heinrich Percy, *ich liebe Sie*." Then I set a match to it. Soon he was replaced by a gorgeous athlete, the star of our local soccer team.

But above all there was Richard Tauber, the most popular and beloved tenor of his time. I adored him.

I looked down on boys my own age. They were

clumsy, sweaty, pimply—and boring. My brother's friends didn't take notice of me. I was Friedl's sister. Cute maybe, but a child. Friedl was my idol. He was a serious young boy, rather quiet, introverted, and five years older than I. He had a fine sense of humor and a great capacity for laughter. Many times I made a pest of myself tagging after him when he wanted to be with his friends or, later on, when he dated. I was supremely happy when the two of us went for a hike, skiing in the nearby mountains, or when he occasionally acted as my chaperon. The pride I felt on being with my handsome brother must have shown on my face every time.

The other favorite member of our family was Grandmother Birnbaum. She was a delicate lady, full of *joie de vivre* and grace. I knew she loved me, maybe more than all her other grandchildren. I cherished the nights when I could sleep at her apartment. It was she who opened the world of music to me. A brilliant pianist, she often gave a recital just for me: Schubert, Chopin, Schumann. Music seemed as necessary to her as breathing. In the early years of my grandparent's marriage, whenever a prominent musician came to Teplitz-Schönau for a recital he was welcomed at the Birnbaum residence. That was at the time when they still had a salon and gave receptions and private concerts in their eight-room apartment.

By the time I introduced Walter to her, her lifestyle had long since changed. My grandfather had died when my mother was only eleven years old, and from then on she had to live in reduced circumstances. I often wished I had known my grandfather, the legendary Robert Birnbaum. His life-size oil portrait dominated my grandmother's dining room: a round, genial man, his beard fashioned in the style of the Emperor Franz Josef. At an early age he had promised himself to become the richest man in Teplitz-Schönau. There was a magnificent ducal mansion called Haus Morave. When my grandfather refused to wear his older brother's hand-me-downs, his mother chided him: "Who do you think you are? The owner of the Morave?" "Not yet," Robert Birnbaum told her loftily, "but one day I will be." And at the age of thirty-two he was.

He was successful with anything he touched. There was first the small textile plant. Then a large rubber factory, which became internationally known, and long after his death was still called the Birnbaum Rubber Company. He traveled all over Europe. Grandmother often pointed to an ornate silver samovar her husband brought back from one of his trips to Russia. The Birnbaum carriages were drawn by four horses, a sign of great wealth!

When he died, in his late forties, my grandmother and her sons were shocked to discover that his business affairs were in a dreadful state. The factories had to be sold to pay off his debts and grandmother had to move to a small apartment. Gone were horses and carriages. Gone was the Haus Morave.

Grandmother, however, went right on trying to squeeze every ounce of enjoyment from her life. She went to the theater, to concerts, carried on with her chamber music soirées and spent a great deal of time with her grandchildren.

My paternal grandfather was also an industrialist. His textile factory was located on the outskirts of town. His youngest son, my father, wanted to study medicine. My father's older brother, Uncle Adolf, was a lawyer, and Uncle Sigmund was a high school teacher. Jenny, his sister, was married and lived in Vienna. My father was the only one still in school and Grandfather Bloch decreed that one day he should take over the factory. And so he did, after his father died.

When World War I broke out, my father volunteered to fight in the Austrian army. A distant relative was summoned to run the business and ran it right into the ground. Undaunted, after returning from the war, my father went back to school and became a public accountant.

We lived on the second floor of a large villa. Linden trees flanked the street. In the back was a garden with raspberry and gooseberry bushes and a variety of fruit trees. I had a sandbox, a swing and an old rusty gazebo where I could play hide and seek. Our apartment was comfortable: heavy oak furniture, a grand piano in the living room, Oriental rugs. My own bedroom was simple. Until I was ten I shared the room with Friedl.

As in any other middle-class home, we had a live-in maid who did the heavy work, such as taking hot embers every winter morning from the kitchen oven to heat the other rooms, each one of which was outfitted with a big tile stove. Those maids usually came from nearby villages, and as a rule stayed with the families for years. My mother would train the girl, teach her how to cook, and after a while just supervise her.

When my parents got married my mother was only nineteen, my father twenty-four. They were deeply in love and nothing changed until they died. My mother was slim, her legs long and beautiful, her eyes large and volatile, and they could darken with anger whenever I disobeyed her. As in most European homes at that time, discipline was very strict. Friedl got the brunt of it. Many times, when I complained about all the rules in our house, he would laugh and say, "You should have been around when I was little." But most of all, there was a great deal of affection from both our parents, to us and to each other. Holding hands, embracing, kissing when leaving or returning, was natural.

My father had a fine sense of humor, which made him laugh at some of the frustrating things in life. He loved music, books and stamps. He owned a valuable stamp collection and belonged to the international philatelic organization. On special occasions we were allowed to leaf through his albums, and he enjoyed explaining the history of his most precious stamps. It was his lifeline to the world, as was the radio set that he built in his spare time. We were awed and proud. Once in a while he let us listen to some far-off station playing music or children's programs.

There were of course periods when we were not happy, when Friedl and I rebelled. At times we resented the monotony of our lives. Every step was regulated: Up at seven, breakfast. School. At noon, our hot meal. Always soup first, which I hated but had to eat. Meat with vegetables and dessert. (Sundays we usually had roast chicken and some fancy dessert.) One-thirty, siesta for my parents; the phone disconnected. At three sharp, black coffee in the salon, and then my father would be off to the office. Four o'clock, a one-hour walk to the ruins of the medieval castle, the Schlossberg. Dinner at seven. Ham, sausage, cheese with tea. To bed at eight-thirty. The soft sound of music from the living room, where our parents would be reading.

There was one thing missing in our family life and that was religion. Although both were Jewish, my parents disliked organized religion of any kind. I was brought up to believe in God, said my prayers every night, and that was all. I did not go to synagogue until I was about twelve years old. When I was little, and we went on our daily walk, my nursemaid would always take me into the Catholic church. There was a tacit understanding between us not to mention it at home. The town and most of its inhabitants were Catholic. The churches, the priests, and many processions through town on the numerous Catholic holidays, the pageantry, the scent of incense, all of it fascinated me. When my mother found out, she put an emphatic stop to my churchgoing. I always knew I was Jewish, but somehow it did not mean much to me until I was in second grade. This was 1927. Liesl, who became my best friend, sat next to me in class. We shared snacks and traded candies and crayons. She had a birthday party and most of the girls in our class were invited. Though I was her best friend, I wasn't. I could not understand it. When I asked her why, she answered, "I'm not allowed to bring Jews to our house." I could see that she, too, was puzzled.

Teplitz-Schönau was very close to the German border, and in 1933, after Hitler came to power, the first Jewish refugees from Germany arrived. The stories they told were frightening. It was at this time that I began to have a strong feeling of wanting to belong to my religion. I decided to go to the synagogue on the High Holidays. Surprisingly, my parents were pleased. I joined a Jewish sports club, Maccabi. By the time Walter and I met, the behavior of the Sudeten Germans, and the anti-Semetic tone of their newspapers had become obvious. Nevertheless, no one believed that what had happened in Germany could possibly happen in Czechoslovakia. There were, of course, people who had their doubts. For instance, my uncle, Herbert Birnbaum, a lifelong Zionist, decided in 1937 to move to Palestine. He had a successful law practice, was the only Jewish council member in our town, and his children were still in school. He uprooted them all and they left. It saved their lives.

After I met Walter in the summer of 1935 my whole life changed. We spent a great deal of time together, hiking in the mountains, alone or with friends. We were happy; we danced, we laughed, we sang, we were untouchable; we were in love.

At the end of the summer my parents decided that it was time for me to prepare myself for a career. My grades in school had been barely passing, and the university was out of the question.

They rightly felt that a girl needed a profession, but did not know what to do with me. Finally it was decided I should learn the hotel business. I was agreeable. It meant I had to move away from home, since the only hotel school was located in Marienbad, a spa about a hundred miles from Teplitz-Schönau. Before I could enroll there, one year of practical experience was required. My father knew the owner of the Hotel Steiner in Prague, who would give me an unpaid job. My greatest dream had been to live in the capital. But most of all, Friedl was in Prague at the university. I went to stay with a Czech family in a room my parents rented for me, worked six days a week for twelve hours a day. But living in Prague was worth anything.

I didn't have much chance to be homesick. I made friends easily and at night went to concerts, the opera, sometimes dancing, and often to the theater. My parents gave me a small monthly allowance, but I managed. Prague was only a three-hour train ride from Teplitz. If I was given a Saturday afternoon off, I would go home and spend a weekend with my family.

Walter, who was in Vienna, and I corresponded regularly. Often I wondered jealously whether he had fallen in love with someone else during our separation. But whenever we saw each other I could tell that he hadn't.

In the fall of 1936 I was ready for school. Marienbad was a beautiful spa, smaller than Teplitz-Schönau. From spring to autumn the town teemed with vacationers. There were countless hotels—some beautiful large ones surrounded by parklike grounds, some smaller pensions. One tree-lined main street had fashionable stores, which were closed off-season. There were elegant restaurants, coffee houses and night clubs. But during fall and winter it was a sleepy small town.

My mother settled me in a rented room and I started school. It was an extensive training in the hotel business. Everything from bookkeeping to cooking, international money exchanges to languages, English and French. My colleagues were mostly pleasant but distant, since I was one of only three Jews in the entire school. Among the local townspeople were many Jewish families and I soon became a member of the community. I found a roommate who was not Jewish, and we became close friends. Gerda was from nearby Karlsbad. Her parents owned a hotel there. They were disgusted that she shared a room with me. Gerda was different from my fellow students. Both of us loved American movies and jazz. Her dream was to travel to foreign countries, as far away as possible from Czechoslovakia or Germany, and she had good reason. Her parents violently disapproved of her engagement to a Jewish boy. They were planning to elope as soon as she was of age. Josh, her boyfriend, already had a job in Prague as a manager in a small hotel. We had a lot in common. We missed our boyfriends, waited for the mailman every day, and made long-distance calls once in a while, a rather complicated procedure at that time.

I was seventeen years old, in love with a boy who loved me, secure with my parents and family nearby, selfish and optimistic enough to be able to enjoy my life. At summer vacation Walter would come home from Vienna. Our only dread was that we would be separated the following September when school started again.

Walter

When I first came to Vienna I was twenty years old. I was overwhelmed by the splendor of the city.

For hours on end I walked the boulevards, past the Hofburg, where the former king-emperors of Austria had lived for centuries, past Baroque churches and the St. Stefan's Dome, past the well-manicured parks, coffeehouses and *Konditoreien*. I would sit on the terrace of the Landman sipping coffee and listening to a string orchestra playing Schubert. I felt intoxicated. This was the life I had dreamed of and soon I would be part of it.

I was accepted at the Max Reinhardt Seminar, the most prestigious acting school in Central Europe. Any graduate could be certain of being offered an engagement in a major German-speaking repertory theater. Even though I was born and raised in Czechoslovakia, my mother tongue was German. I had been educated in German-speaking schools. It was the language we spoke at home.

From the moment I was accepted at the school, a strict regime kept me busy from morning to night. The curriculum included lessons in elocution, singing, dancing, fencing, stage direction, designing and lighting. But most important of all were rehearsals of scenes to be performed for the faculty.

Reinhardt's Baroque Schlosstheater was situated in the middle of the lush, well-groomed park of Schönbrunn. Several times during the school year we appeared on the stage before an invited audience. Most of us chose stage names. I wanted to keep my first name and initials. I called myself Walter Kent.

I auditioned for a part in Molnár's *The Play's the Thing* and got the role.

For weeks I worked furiously, to prepare myself for opening night. Then I waited up all night for the reviews. The most feared drama critic in Vienna wrote: "Walter Kent gave a finely honed performance." I carried that newspaper clipping in my wallet until it finally disintegrated years later.

For a short time I fancied myself in love with another girl. Her name was Susan Mitchell and she was the one American student among the female contingent at the Reinhardt School. She was also the only one who drove a Mercedes, a fiery red convertible. With her free-flowing blond hair, she looked like Ginger Rogers. Her accent was delightful, and the whole class applauded when she gave a rendition of the monologue of Shaw's *Joan of Arc* in German. A wild scramble began when we read for a student performance of Arthur Schnitzler's *Liebelei*. Who would be chosen to play opposite her in that passionate love story?

I didn't get the part, perhaps because I had none of the attributes of a leading man. Nevertheless, my moment of glory came midsemester when one of our professors had the bizarre idea of using those few students who spoke English to stage Galsworthy's *The First and the Last,* in the original English.

My English lessons with Miss Williams, an old Scottish spinster who had settled in Teplitz many years ago, paid off. I got the part of a prosecutor whose younger brother is accused of murder. Susan Mitchell played a prostitute. She asked me to continue rehearsing after school in her flat, where she lived with an aunt.

Then one night Susan showed me the snapshot of a young American—athletic, blond, tall, and as I found out, rich. She was very fond of him.

Rehearsals continued. Everyone seemed to be doing well, but my performance got worse. Susan had to correct me constantly. I was, I assume, in love. On opening night, shortly before curtain time, I seemed to have lost my voice. There was a knock at the door: "Ten minutes." The cast took turns looking through the peephole. The house was sold out. In the third row I could see Susan's aunt. She talked animatedly to her escort, the young blond man in the photograph. That was the final stroke. My voice came back and I got through the evening, somehow. The applause was generous.

Susan's aunt had made arrangements for a party afterward in one of the places where the potent new wine of the season, Heuriger, was served. I wanted to snub my rival, but he had such a disarming smile and he held Susan's hand so unselfconsciously that I caught myself actually liking him. By the time we had finished the third bottle of Heuriger we were embracing each other. It was a wonderful evening; I had lost my imaginary love but gained a friend.

We stayed up until morning to read the reviews in the newspapers. They were catastrophic. One reviewer observed that German actors would be well advised to act in plays written in their own tongue. Susan garnered only two words: "Bloody amateur." I didn't fare much better. She failed to appear in class on Monday. Around noon I called her aunt, who told me that Susan had left town.

A few days later I got a phone call from my mother. My father had died of a massive stroke. The next day I was on the train to Teplitz. Our father was beloved, and not only in our town. He had friends all over the world, even in America, which he had visited in 1921. It seemed inconceivable that this ebullient, lusty, healthy man was gone forever. Practically all of Teplitz, Jew and non-Jew alike, turned out to honor him.

I stayed a few more days with my mother but had to leave for Vienna to go on with my studies at the seminar.

As time went on, I was given bigger and better parts. At the end of the second year we prepared for our final exams. We had to be well-briefed on the history of the theater, had to recite three monologues and had to stage scenes from the classics as well as from modern dramatic literature. The panel of examiners were prominent actors and directors.

When it was my turn I went into shock. There in the audience sat Max Reinhardt. He was one of the judges. An unbending perfectionist, he demanded impeccable performances from his students.

Stage fright, we were told, was as predictable as

the disastrous dress rehearsal where everything goes haywire. For a few seconds I froze. But then I looked straight at the master and I acted for *him* . . . and must have acted well enough. The following day I was the possessor of the all-important *Bühnenbuch*, the certificate that permitted me to become a member of the actor's union. I was entitled to accept employment on any of the German-speaking stages of Austria, Switzerland and Czechoslovakia.

There were some lucky ones—spotted by agents in previous performances—who were hired for theaters in Berlin, Munich, Prague, Vienna and Zurich. But for a Jewish actor like me, Germany was off-limits. In 1937 the German stage was *judenrein* (purged of Jews). But most of us were looking for a place in one of the smaller repertory theaters in the provinces. I considered myself lucky when the director of a small Sudeten German repertory theater in Czechoslovakia offered me a contract.

The small town of Leitmeritz had its own municipal theater. The interior was Baroque, with the traditional red velvet seats, the loges, the huge chandelier. It had a seating capacity of five hundred. For a provincial town, it was quite respectable.

I was the youngest of a company of actors and actresses, all professionals. They had been in and out of various repertory companies and were well-rehearsed in a variety of roles. This year attention centered around a new leading man. Besides me, he was the only Jewish member of the company.

Leitmeritz was quite a comedown for Mathias Wieland. He had played many of the major stages

of Germany and had been a highly respected char-
acter actor on the stage, as well as in motion pictures.
The day Hitler seized power, Wieland's career in
Germany was finished. He was glad to have found
any kind of engagement, and the intellectual community of Leitmeritz was treated to some of the most
memorable performances in the history of their
theater.

The work was hard. A different play or operetta
opened almost every week. If there was a free hour,
I spent it at the coffeehouse on the main square. As
in any other small town, this was the focal point of
social life. Here newspapers were read, letters composed, endless chess games fought. Here love affairs
started and here they died.

A couple of times Hanna sneaked out of school
and took the train from Marienbad to Leitmeritz, a
three-hour ride. She would arrive late Friday evening
and stay at a small hotel near the theater.

On New Year's Eve of 1937 I appeared in a popular
comedy called *Why Do You Lie, Chérie?* We played
to a capacity audience. Hanna sat in the fourth row.
There was something like an ovation for me when the
final curtain came down. Then the elite of Leitmeritz
dispersed to welcome the New Year into their homes.

I checked my watch. It was eleven. The last train
for Teplitz would leave in half an hour. We could
still make it. I knew Hanna would be waiting at the
stage door.

I had a glass of champagne with my colleagues,
grabbed a bottle and two glasses, and rushed toward
the exit. I didn't even bother to remove my make-up.

Hanna and I ran in the direction of the station. It

had started snowing. The platform was deserted. Breathless, laughing, hugging each other, we had just enough time to get our tickets. The train steamed into the station. We jumped up the steps to a first-class compartment. The whole train was empty.

There was a knock on the door. It was the conductor. "Only five minutes to midnight," he said, punching our tickets. With a smile, he glanced longingly at the champagne bottle, which lay unopened on the soft seat.

"How about having a glass of champagne to greet the New Year?" Hanna asked him.

He seemed tempted.

"One moment," he said, disappeared and returned immediately with a thermos bottle. He unscrewed the top and I poured the champagne into his tin cup. Then I filled our own glasses and we welcomed 1938.

By the time we arrived in Teplitz it was snowing heavily. We walked the short distance from the station to my mother's home. The house was dark.

We tiptoed up to the second floor to my room and sat down on the couch; I turned on the radio.

"This is Jack Hilton from the Savoy Hotel in London, wishing you all a very Happy New Year and signing off with 'Good Night, Sweetheart.' " It was his theme song, which we had heard many times in the past.

That night in Teplitz we were lovers for the first time.

Two months later, on March 12, 1938, Hitler invaded Austria. The Anschluss had instant repercussions.

Prominent Austrian Jewish personalities, among

them writers and musicians, had been arrested and sent to concentration camps. Escape across the border to Czechoslovakia was becoming increasingly difficult.

Mathias Wieland and I met at the coffeehouse to discuss the political situation. We both felt that the Anschluss was only the beginning. What would happen next? Where should we turn? Coffeehouse friends who had so recently welcomed us to their *Stammtisch* —a patron's special table—turned their heads. We felt ostracized and trapped.

Already for a number of years in all the cities, townships and even villages in the Sudetenland, the Germans had been organizing the SDP (Sudetendeutsche Partei), a local version of the National Socialist Party in Germany. The Czech government failed to crush the movement. Beginning in May, the director Albert Rudolph scheduled the premiere of a play by a new German writer—a work of pure Nazi propaganda—forced upon him by the Sudeten German party of Leitmeritz. Wieland was assigned the leading role. Even though there was no one else in the ensemble who could have played the part, he refused to accept it. Only a few hours after he had walked out of the director's office, he received a visit from a high functionary of the Sudeten German party.

Quite bluntly Wieland was given to understand that rigorous measures would be taken against his aged parents, who still lived in Germany. Wieland reconsidered and played the part.

I almost shared the stage with him. But Rudolph informed me that I was not quite well-suited for the part of a young German cadet in the same play.

Hoping that I would understand, he terminated my contract, which should have run for two more months.

I saw Wieland once more, a few months later, in Prague. He was on his way to America.

Hanna

In the spring of 1938 I had graduated from the hotel management school in Marienbad. I was immediately offered a position as a hostess in the famous garden restaurant Geysirpark in Karlsbad, about one hundred miles from Teplitz-Schönau.

Karlsbad was like a fairyland. Day and night, life seemed to bubble forth like the gushing geyser in the enormous glass arcade where health-seekers from all over the world strolled up and down, sipping the warm waters while the *Kurorchester* played medleys by Strauss and Rossini. Miracles of healing were ascribed to Karlsbad. Luxurious hotels, like the Grand Hotel Pupp, welcomed Arabian sheiks, Persian millionaires, American film magnates and German industrialists. At the beginning of the season, swank shops like Cartier of Paris or Braun of Vienna opened their doors for the three summer months.

A normal Karlsbad day started early in the morning and was organized strictly around the water ritual. There was a strenuous routine of drinking the healing waters and taking the baths before breakfast that had to be obeyed and carried through with moral fortitude. The rewards came in the afternoon, when the *"Regime"* was discarded. Hotels offered a five o'clock *thé dansant*, complete with pastries and sandwiches, and cakes topped with mountains of whipped cream. Middle-aged women, overweight men, gigolos and pretty girls mingled, danced, flirted and arranged dates for the evening. Night clubs flourished. The local theater played operettas by Kálmán and Léhar. And there were a few establishments devoted to gambling as well as to the world's oldest profession.

This was the Karlsbad known the world over, the Karlsbad I had heard about and read about; a place where every day was a holiday—or so I had imagined.

But that wasn't the Karlsbad of 1938. That summer I stood at my post at the Geysirpark waiting for the captains and kings of the world to make their grandiose entrances. I waited in vain. A few people still arrived to take the cure, but most of the exotic contingent that gave Karlsbad its allure stayed away that summer. The political climate was forbidding. There were enough Germans enjoying the pleasures of Karlsbad, but they didn't frequent the posh shops that were geared for the international clientele. The Sudeten German Karlsbaders, who before the start of the season had tramped through the streets and parks of the spa singing boisterous and provocative songs imported from across the border, now put on their "international" face. After all, this was the season. The "dear guest," even if Jewish, had to be pampered, at least until the summer was over.

But even though the Nazis were hibernating, even though the weather was mild and pleasant, something undefinable and ominous was in the air.

Although emigration had become difficult, more and more of our friends had been talking about leaving Czechoslovakia. Many German Jews had left Europe during the last few years. Now, since the Germans had marched into Austria, Austrian refugees were also looking for asylum.

The United States was the most sought-after country. In order to immigrate to America an affidavit was required, an official document from an American citizen who would assume full financial responsibility for the immigrant. Only after it was approved by the U.S. State Department would the applicant be eligible for a quota number. The U.S. government supplied all countries with a fixed amount of quota numbers for immigration visas. The Czech quota was small. By 1938 it was oversubscribed for a number of years. The exceptions were blood relatives of U.S. citizens, who would be issued special visas. Walter's brother Paul had taken care of all the necessary papers for him and his mother.

Walter, who was staying with his mother in Teplitz, came to visit as often as he could.

He would pick me up in the afternoon when my work was finished, and we would take long walks through the woods and parks. The American consulate had notified him to expect his visa any day. He hated the thought of leaving me. He was afraid of America. His brothers, in their letters, told him flatly that he would have no chance of finding work as an actor. How could he ever tell them he was engaged to be married and that he would like to bring me along? Naturally, we discussed all of this endlessly. The only solution seemed to be that he must leave as soon as he had all the necessary documents. Once settled in Los Angeles, he would send for me.

At the same time, we, like thousands of others, were still optimistic: maybe Germany would not invade the Czech republic and we could stay there with our families.

In mid-August the newspapers announced the arrival of Lord Runciman, a member of the British Parliament, an emissary of England's Prime Minister Neville Chamberlain. Together with President Beneš and the members of his administration, Runciman would discuss the problem of the Sudeten and hopefully settle it. Never would our allies sell us out!

About 300,000 German-speaking Czechs lived in the Sudeten, an area that for hundreds of years had belonged to the Kingdom of Bohemia. The Germans had always been a minority. They lived well and prospered, and got along with the ruling class. They also hated the Czechs and were inveterate anti-Semites. Konrad Henlein, a former bank clerk, had organized the SDP years before, and under his leadership the Sudeten German Nazis had managed to stir up unrest among the population. To "save his German subjects" Hitler now demanded that the Sudeten should become part of Grossdeutschland—his Greater Germany. Every true Sudeten German was screaming Hitler's slogan, *Heim in's Reich* (Back home to the Fatherland), ignoring completely the fact that the Sudeten had never been a part of Germany but had belonged to the Austrian Empire before World War I.

Anxiously we followed Runciman's every move. After Prague he traveled through some of the Sudeten

German cities, accompanied by Henlein. We read about the hunting trips he took with the landed gentry, all Nazis and often aristocrats like Clary-Aldringen, whom he visited in Teplitz-Schönau. It was a bad omen.

A few weeks later Chamberlain flew to Munich, and on September 30, 1938, our Allies sold out Czechoslovakia: Hitler had won another bloodless victory. The republic, well armed and willing to fight, was forced to surrender the Sudetenland to Germany, and did so because Chamberlain reassured it and the world that the annexation of the Sudetenland would be Hitler's last territorial demand; Hitler had solemnly promised not to violate the new Czech borders. After his return to England, Chamberlain claimed that he had achieved "peace in our time."

We were homeless overnight.

By the end of September, Karlsbad was all but deserted. I returned to my family in Teplitz. Walter and I helped my parents pack for our move to Prague. We were not going to wait until the Germans marched in. I could no longer hide behind my selfish and childlike ignorance. I watched as my parents' faces became saddened and worried. My father, as always, was calm and positive. He tried to convince us that once in Prague he would be able to find work and a place for us to live. He withdrew whatever money there was from the bank. A moving company loaded our furniture on a truck. Friedl, who had come from Prague to help, supervised the transport. Our two canaries, Hansel and Matzel, went to an old charwoman who used to do the extra-heavy work at spring and fall cleanings. She had been with our family for many years and was decent and faithful. She cried bitterly. My mother gave all her plants to a non-Jewish friend. Our maid, Betty, sobbed through the entire day of packing: she begged my parents to take her along. She'd stay with us without pay. It was impossible, of course. We were going to store our furniture in a Prague warehouse until we could find an apartment. Very few of our non-Jewish acquaintances showed any sign of compassion. The rest of the Sudeten German citizens were jubilant. They would finally become Germans; they displayed their disdain for us openly on the streets and in stores. The same exodus occurred throughout the Sudetenland. Jewish as well as Czech families moved into the inner part of the country. Most of them went to Prague.

Aware of what was happening in Austria, most of the Jewish community of Teplitz fled within weeks; it numbered almost five thousand people, among them families who had their roots in the old town for hundreds of years. A few decided to stay. We left behind our grandmother, Helene Birnbaum, then close to eighty. "This is my home," she said. "What could they possibly do to an old woman like me?"

It was a gray September afternoon when we closed the door to our home for the last time. We carried our suitcases to the station, accompanied only by Walter and our crying maid; we tried not to turn around and look at the nearby mountains that we loved so much.

The express was bursting with refugees. We were able to get one seat for my mother, and my father,

Friedl and I stood in the passageway. Through the train windows we watched the familiar landscape fading away.

In Prague we looked for a place to live. The city was overflowing with refugees. After staying in Friedl's room for a few days, my parents and I found a miserable little hotel. There were two beds with a nightstand on each side, a hideous brown dresser, and a bathroom down the hall that had to be shared with the other occupants of the floor. For our family, that shabby room became home.

Friedl was to start his last semester of medical school. However, the Munich Pact included the take-over of the famous old German Charles University and Medical School in Prague. The Germans insisted that it was part of the Sudeten and a German cultural center, and would therefore fall under German juris-diction. Jewish members of the faculty were dis-charged. Jewish students were no longer allowed to enroll or to continue with their studies.

The fall was foggy and wet. People huddled in coffeehouses, hatching fantastic plans. Shoddy char-acters took advantage of the refugees' plight and promised them visas to countries never heard of in our part of the world: Venezuela—the Dominican Republic—Cuba—Honduras.

The population of Prague accepted our presence reluctantly. To most Czechs we were Germans, and we were hated and despised as such. Also we were Jews.

Walter had come to Prague to be with me. One afternoon I found the room I shared with my parents deserted. There was a note on the desk, obviously scribbled in haste.

Hanna,
    The police took us to the railway station. Our application for residency has been refused. We are to be sent back to Teplitz. Friedl went with us to the station.
                                      Goodbye.

I turned around and raced to Walter's hotel. It was nearby, and luckily Walter was still there. We were at the railway station within a few minutes.

All the waiting rooms were roped off. Through the window I finally spotted my parents among the hundreds who had been rounded up for the same reason. After hours of desperate waiting, everyone was released. It was midnight before we could return to our hotel. For the first time in my life I saw tears in my father's eyes.

Walter

One morning early in October, Herr Schindler, who had delivered the daily mail, telegrams and packages to our house for many years brought a registered letter from the American consulate in Prague. "I hope you're not going to leave us," Herr Schindler said.

My mother and I had been granted our visas and we were to present ourselves upon receipt of the letter at the American consulate in Prague.

I was overjoyed, but my mother refused to leave. She had decided to stay in Teplitz, in the old house where she had lived all her life, and where everyone knew her. She wanted to be close to her sister Clara and her brother Rudolph. Here she had lived happily with my father. Here her three sons were born. She felt too old to be uprooted and become dependent on her children in a strange, faraway country. All my pleas to make her see the gravity of the situation were futile. She wouldn't even consider making the move to Prague, which most of her friends had done.

All over Teplitz, swastikas began to appear. Most of the Jewish merchants had closed their stores. The rabbi of our congregation, who had prepared me for my bar mitzvah, asked me to help him remove the

Torah scrolls from the tabernacle. Outside the temple a member of our congregation was waiting to drive the car with the scrolls to Prague. There, we assumed, they would be safe.

The most obvious change took place in the streets and parks. Former classmates looked the other way when I made an effort to greet them. Herr Hammer, who had known me all my life, and from whom I had learned how to operate the projection machine in my father's theater, ignored me. On his face he wore a smirk. On his left arm he wore a large swastika.

It was time to leave.

Immediately after my arrival in Prague I went to the American consulate. As I approached the building I saw a long line of people stretching around two blocks. A terrible sadness pervaded their faces as they patiently awaited their turn to submit their applications for immigration visas.

After waiting for hours, I presented my registered letter to the guard at the entrance and was ushered into a room where an official routinely looked through my papers and routinely stamped the American visa into my Czechoslovakian passport.

It was that simple.

I ran all the way to Hanna's hotel and together we studied the passport and the American stamp that would open the door to freedom. To celebrate the miracle I took Hanna to a restaurant and we got slightly tipsy on a bottle of wine. After lunch I went to a travel office and was able to book a flight to London for October 28. That would give us two weeks to ourselves.

Meanwhile, Prague the Golden City became Prague

the Gray City. On street corners, under the arcades of the old town square, in narrow passageways, people clustered, talking in hushed voices—refugees, unwelcome guests, speaking an unwelcome language. Every morning new rumors were in the air, to be replaced the next morning by more new rumors.

Long lines formed in front of the main post office. People waited their turn to search the pages of the only existing New York phone directory in the hope of finding, if not known relatives, at least a namesake to whom they could write asking for help. And curiously, some of those desperate efforts to save their lives were successful.

Hanna and I walked a great deal, holding hands, talking, making plans. I assured her that once in America, once in Hollywood, I would do everything to get her a visa. I also would see to it that her family could join us. Of course the thought occurred to me that we could get married right away. But I was scared. What would my brothers say if I arrived in Hollywood with a wife. They had never heard of Hanna. It would be terribly difficult for me, setting out to earn a living in a new country with a new language. How would I find work, any work? My brothers might have to support me.

One day all those unspoken fears and doubts sprang up, broke open. We stood in the rain on the Charles Bridge. Hanna instinctively guessed my ambiguous feelings, my mental turmoil, and it was she who shared them and gave me courage. She would wait. There wouldn't be any war. She and her family would settle down in Prague, like so many other Jewish families. Why shouldn't they feel secure in the Czech republic? Hitler would never dare to cross the border, what with England and France as our allies. I was grateful that she understood. I embraced her and our tears mingled with the rain that poured down from a melancholy sky.

I had rented a room in a sleazy hotel frequented by streetwalkers and their customers. Unlike other hotels this one did not require police registration: There was still the possibility the Czech army might induct me at the last minute and prevent me from leaving.

Our last night together was one of grim despair. The room was drab and airless. A bed, a washstand, torn curtains, a small window facing the dark-brown wall of the next building. The odor of thousands of previous occupants seemed to have impregnated everything. Sleepless, we huddled together under a dirty blanket, waiting for the morning.

We got up early and checked out. There was still an hour's time before I could board the bus to the airport. In a thick fog we crossed the street and found a coffeehouse. Silently we stirred our coffee. We had said everything during the night. In Hanna's eyes I could see her dread of being left alone. I looked away, looked at my wristwatch. There was still half an hour. I wished it was over.

"Beautiful suit," Hanna said, and her hand tenderly caressed the material of the new suit I wore. A new suit for the new world.

I smiled with embarrassment. Again I checked my watch. "It's time," I said, and paid for our uneaten breakfast.

When we got to the airport office on Wenceslas Square the bus had just arrived. Still a few more minutes. We stood on the sidewalk, holding hands. Hanna started crying softly. The driver was honking the horn. We held on to each other in a last embrace.

I boarded the bus. Through the fogged-up window I saw her standing alone in the rain.

Walter

The CLT 40 was a small plane of the Czech Airline. I looked out of the window after we took off. Below, Prague was hardly discernible. Hanna was somewhere down there.

I had traveled abroad in the past to Norway, Germany and Austria, but always by train or boat, and usually with my family. This was my first flight. I was scared. Anxiously I looked not only at my fellow travelers, but also watched the behavior of the pretty stewardess who walked up and down the aisle. I scrutinized her face for any sign of an impending catastrophe.

Sitting next to me was an elderly lady who continuously opened her purse, searching for something. I felt her worried glance and smiled encouragingly at her. She told me she was going to London to live with her sister. She had sold all her possessions, even her precious Steinway, to raise the money for the trip. "I hope the plane is safe," she said. "It's my first flight."

She reminded me of my mother, who could have been sitting right next to me if she hadn't stubbornly insisted on staying in Teplitz.

There were about forty passengers, all upper-middle class, who obviously had been fortunate enough to get a visa to a foreign country.

Lunch was served. There was a small red, white and blue flag on my plate. It was October 28, Czechoslovakia's Independence Day.

The Czech pilot announced that we were flying over the Rhine and could see the Lorelei rock. Few of the passengers bothered to look.

After a four-hour flight the plane landed in London. I spent the night with friends, who drove me the next morning to Southampton, where I embarked the S.S. *Roosevelt*, which was filled with refugees escaping Hitler. I shared a second-class cabin with three others. From open cabin doors one could hear snatches of conversation in Czech, Polish, Hungarian and German. I spent most of the days on deck, preferring the bracing cold wind to the confines of my cabin, where one roommate, a young German, moaned and thrashed on his bunk in seasick misery. The other two spoke only Polish. As the days went by, fewer and fewer passengers appeared for their meals.

In the dining room I sat next to a Mr. and Mrs. Wright and their twenty-year-old daughter, Nancy. They had been on a vacation trip visiting Germany and had been charmed by the Black Forest, the Rhine and the friendliness of the German people.

"What are you going to do in America, Walter?"

"I am emigrating to America," I said, "because I am a Jew, and as a Jew, Mr. Wright, there is no future for me in Europe."

"I cannot quite believe it," Mr. Wright said uncomfortably.

"Haven't you heard of anti-Semitism?"

"Ah, yes." He emptied his wine glass. "You'll find anti-Semitism everywhere, Walter. Even in America. Now, I personally have no prejudice against Jews. But then, I hardly know any, except for my lawyer. He's as smart as they come. It's a pity I can't bring him to my club."

"Why not?" I asked naïvely.

"It's restricted; but then, he wouldn't have felt comfortable there anyway. Well," Mr. Wright raised his glass, "here's to you, Walter, and to your success in America."

All my knowledge of America had come through the movies and from my brothers' letters.

Now I was in New York and everything was different. The skyscrapers, the traffic and the throngs of people rushing along the sidewalk made me dizzy. There was a heat wave, supposedly unheard of for early November. Indian Summer, they called it. My shirt clung to my skin as I walked the streets.

For six days and nights I traveled across the continent on a Greyhound bus. I had never imagined such farmland, which seemed to stretch on forever. My idea of the West was quite different from what I had expected. As a youngster I had devoured the books of Karl May, a famous German author who wrote about the Wild West. His characters, Winnetou and Old Shatterhand, were household words. He described the plains, rivers, mountain ranges, Indian tribes and cowboys in the most vivid fashion. I learned later that Karl May had never set foot outside his small German hometown.

At last the bus pulled into the large terminal in

downtown Los Angeles. Tired and dirty, I climbed down. There they were, my brothers Paul and Fritz, wonderfully familiar, although I hadn't seen them for three years, yet also different with their healthy suntans and colorful sports coats. We hugged.

Paul put my suitcase in the trunk of his Cadillac and started the car. As we drove I told my brothers about our mother's insistence on staying in Teplitz, the whereabouts of other relatives, and explained to them what was really happening in Czechoslovakia.

"What are my chances as an actor?" I finally asked.

"It'll be very difficult in the beginning," Fritz said guardedly.

Paul concentrated on his driving and didn't say a word.

"You'll find you have plenty of company," Fritz said. "Hollywood is full of refugee actors."

Paul added, "The best actors, directors, writers and composers in the world are arriving every day. We have a regular European film colony."

Obviously my brothers were trying to tell me that finding work as an actor would be quite impossible. But it was Hanna who was uppermost in my mind. I had promised to get her out of Europe, and I swore to myself I would.

It was quite natural that I appealed first to my brothers for help. I needed a sponsor for Hanna's affidavit.

They told me they had already overextended themselves for family and friends. I also learned that their position in the motion picture industry was rather tenuous. Fritz, who three years before had arrived with his family from London, was a free-lance writer. Since English was not his mother tongue, he carried the label "Continental" writer, meaning that he always had to work with an American, an unsatisfactory and often frustrating arrangement.

The vagaries of Hollywood had also affected Paul. His career in motion pictures had started right after the end of World War I, when he worked as a cub reporter for our father's film magazine, the *Filmschau*. One summer day in 1921 he was dispatched to Karlsbad to interview an illustrious visitor from faraway California, a Hollywood nabob. Carl Laemmle, the president of Universal Pictures, had come to the spa to take the healing waters and had refused to give any interviews. He wanted to rest. But Paul found a way to meet the tycoon face to face. What followed was the longest interview on record. When Paul finally felt he had worn out his welcome, Laemmle offered him a job in his main office in New York. Without hesitation, Paul accepted.

He started as an office boy at Universal, was transferred to Hollywood, and wound up a full-fledged producer. But suddenly and unexpectedly Laemmle sold his studio, and Paul lost his job.

Eventually he joined Metro-Goldwyn-Mayer, the most prestigious studio at the time. His first production was not successful, and only a short while before I arrived, he had been handed the dreaded pink slip.

A man of little patience, he had decided to apply his talents to another field of activity in the sprawling movie industry. He opened a talent agency. Not wanting to disappoint and alarm the family, he had kept us in ignorance of this change.

The beginning was rough; he was now a salesman instead of a producer-buyer. But during his years as a producer he had made many friends. Actors remembered the producer who always had words of cheer and encouragement for them even if he didn't have a role to offer. Writers remembered his admiration and respect for their work. And some of them—for it was the time when not every creative artist had an agent—chose him as their representative.

November felt like spring. The chirping of birds and the exotic fragrance of flowers filled the air. Palm trees towered over charming tile-roofed stucco houses. Bright sunshine poured from the spacious sky into the upstairs studio of Fritz's rambling Spanish home. I jumped out of bed and threw open the doors to the balcony.

The welcome aroma of fresh coffee rose from the kitchen downstairs. I was whistling happily, filled again with my usual optimism and self-confidence. How could things not work out in this paradise?

Fritz and my sister-in-law, Mimi, were sitting at the table when I came into the kitchen. At the sight of their faces, I stopped. Something was wrong. Fritz wordlessly showed me the morning paper.

It was November 10, 1938. Reinhard Heydrich, then chief of the Gestapo, in retribution for the assassination of a secretary at the German embassy in Paris by a young Polish Jew named Herschel Grynszpan, had ordered the burning of all synagogues in Germany, Austria and the Sudetenland. Thousands of Jews had been arrested and thrown into concentration camps, their houses had been broken into and ransacked. Crudely painted swastikas appeared on Jewish-owned shops, windows were smashed, streets littered with broken glass. The *Kristallnacht*, the papers called it.

My first thought was my mother. Could they possibly harm a sixty-year-old lady? Of course, I knew Prague wasn't occupied by the Germans, so Hanna and her family were safe. I felt guilty that I was so far away and ashamed to be glad that I was out of Europe.

I wrote to Hanna every day. I told her that I was happy, that I would soon find work, that I missed her terribly and was confident of being able to send her an affidavit as well as the money to get her out of Europe.

Weeks went by. Nothing happened. Again I turned to my brothers. I needed work, I told them, needed it desperately, if not as an actor, which I realized might be impossible, then at least as an errand boy—anything. Paul, with all his connections, could make a phone call—that's all, I thought, that was necessary.

A few days later I heard from him.

"You said you would even take a job as an office boy," Paul said. "Well, you've got it. Report Monday morning at Columbia Studios."

Monday morning I entered a Hollywood studio for the first time: Columbia Pictures on Gower Street. The moment the familiar odor of backstage filled my nostrils I knew I was home.

My job was not exactly glamorous, and at twenty-four I may have been a little old for it. But it was a job and I fulfilled my duties to the best of my abilities. First thing in the morning I had to deliver mail to some fifty-odd departments. In the afternoon I took coffee from the commissary to writers, directors and producers. Frequently I was asked to sit down and discuss the political situation in Europe.

The best day was Friday—payday, $15 a week, quite a respectable salary in those days.

Luck, it seemed, was coming my way.

Hanna

We had Dutch relatives on my mother's side whom I had never met before. Cousin Martha lived with her husband Johann and two small children in Naarden-Bussum, a suburb of Amsterdam. She knew about our problems and offered to hire me as a housekeeper. I had to sign a one-year contract. But Cousin Martha's letter didn't mean what it said. What they really needed was a maid.

Traditionally Holland had given asylum to countless refugees. But in the fall of 1938 the Dutch government had closed its borders to immigrants. There was one exception: household help who had secured a position prior to their arrival. The contract was only for me; the rest of my family was not included. I did not want to be separated from my parents. However, after long discussions, they convinced me that once in Holland, I might find a way for them to join me. Before Walter left he had suggested it might be easier to get my visa at the American consulate in Rotterdam.

The Dutch visa arrived. My suitcases were packed. I prayed that something might happen at the last minute to prevent me from leaving.

It was November 6, 1938.

A taxi was waiting in front of the hotel. My brother

and father carried down my luggage. For a few moments my mother and I were alone in the room. Quickly she took her fur coat out of the closet. "Please take it—I want you to have it."

The black sealskin coat had fitted her elegant figure superbly. It was her most precious possession. I protested that I could not accept the coat. But she insisted, and I had to give in.

On the ride to the airport Friedl made a few lame jokes. We tried to be as casual as if I were going back to school. We kissed and hugged. I climbed the few steps to the plane. Once more I turned around. My father, his arms around my mother and brother, waved his handkerchief.

In Rotterdam I had to change planes. There were no waiting rooms, just an open platform. Rain came down heavily. In my mother's coat I felt like a wet black animal whose fur had gotten too large for its skinny body.

My relatives were waiting for me at the Amsterdam airport. They were younger than my parents. I couldn't find any family resemblance in Martha's face. Johann, tall and stocky, shook my hand heartily. They seemed glad to see me. We had no language problem; all of us spoke German fluently. Naarden-Bussum was about twenty miles outside Amsterdam. The taxi stopped in a street with identical three-story houses. Johann and Martha helped me up the stairs with the suitcases.

The attic room had a dormer window that looked out onto the street. It was clean but melancholy, its sadness intensified by a light bulb hanging from the ceiling, a blue paper shade attached to it crookedly.

Wet and cold, I sat down on the unmade bed. What was I doing here? How could I have made this choice? I fought my tears. What a terrible impression I would make if someone walked in now. I started to unpack. On top of my suitcase, neatly framed, were the photographs of my parents, and one of Walter. Quickly I closed the top again. I was not ready to look at them yet.

I hung up my mother's wet coat and washed my face. The door opened slowly. Two small children stood there staring at me with grave, curious faces. Antje was six years old; she had dark hair, dark eyes, and somewhat resembled Martha; Jaap, a year younger, was cute and skinny.

They did not understand German. We shook hands gravely. For a moment they both giggled, then ran down the stairs.

The next morning Martha took me all over the house, explaining my duties. Was all this expected of me? I was a healthy, strong nineteen-year-old. However, I had no idea about housekeeping; we had always had a maid at home. I also realized very quickly that my relatives did not consider me "family." I would have to eat alone in the kitchen—after I served their dinner. I had to bathe the children, take them to school in the morning and sometimes do the marketing. My day started at six and ended late in the evening when all the chores were done. Every second Sunday and second Tuesday I had a day off. My monthly salary was 25 guilders, the equivalent of $20.

Naarden-Bussum was a joyless suburb. Most people commuted to Amsterdam daily, as did Johann, who worked at the American Express office. He left by train in the morning and returned in the evening. On my days off, I would also go to Amsterdam. I always felt happier in the big city. I would go to a concert, the museum or just walk along the streets. My Dutch slowly improved. But I was desperately lonely.

Martha and Johann were unwilling to make even the slightest effort to help my family. They felt I greatly exaggerated the problem—and besides, what could they do? Johann suggested that perhaps the Refugee Committee in Amsterdam might be of assistance.

On my first day off, I went there. The anteroom was crowded. When my turn came I met Dr. Pick, a Jewish lawyer from Berlin. His listened to my story, then interrupted me before I could finish.

"Miss Bloch, do you see these stacks of files?" He pointed to documents piled high against the wall. "Those are requests from residents all over Holland for visas for their families. The Dutch government refuses to grant any more entry permits. If your parents had a substantial bank account here and could prove to be self-supporting, they might have a chance to get a visitor's visa, which could be extended. Otherwise it is hopeless."

I got up and started to leave.

"Let me warn you about one thing," Dr. Pick called after me. "If your parents should try to cross the border from Germany illegally, as others have done lately, the border guards will send them to a camp for illegal refugees, Camp Westerbork. I would

not recommend it, not even to your brother, who is
a young man."

Every morning I waited anxiously for the mail. My
parents' letters were full of news about relatives and
friends. Uncle Adolf, my father's oldest brother, had
committed suicide in Prague. He was the celebrity
in our family. A lawyer, he had become president of
a large insurance company in Vienna. He was rich,
well-known in government and social circles. His
non-Jewish wife and son had remained in Vienna.

My old grandmother had stayed in Teplitz. Everyone in town knew and admired her. Now the Nazis
had forced her out of her apartment, where she had
lived for thirty years. Her housekeeper, who had
been with her all her life, had left her. She said she
was a good German and would not work for Jews
any longer.

Uncle Sigmund, my father's other brother, a high
school teacher, had been dismissed. The Steiners, our
oldest friends, had finally received their visas to England.

My parents and Friedl had found an apartment in
Prague. My father worked as a bookkeeper in a factory. Friedl was employed at the Kultusgemeinde,
the Jewish Community Center in Prague.

Late one evening I sat in my room reading *Gone
With the Wind*. The house was still. The doorbell
rang. It rarely happened that unannounced visitors
called so late. I rushed downstairs. Martha was already at the door talking to the mailman. "It's for
you, Hanna, a special delivery letter."

I immediately recognized Walter's handwriting and tore open the envelope while walking up to my room. With one foot I shut the door and sat on the bed.

Walter had found someone willing to give me an affidavit. The papers were going to be sent directly to the American consulate in Rotterdam, and I would be sent a copy.

I could not believe it. After only four weeks in America he had done it. I started to laugh. Then I read the letter for a second time, more slowly. How absolutely marvelous. I stretched out on my bed, pressing the letter close to me. Suddenly the attic room was not so cold. I looked at the framed photographs of my parents. They would be so happy to hear the good news. It might be impossible to get my family and Friedl into Holland, but once in America, I would be able to help them.

It was getting late. I undressed quickly and got under the covers. I felt wide awake and full of high hopes. I read the letter once more. As soon as the affidavit arrived I wound go to see the consul in Rotterdam. The letter was postmarked December 5; today was the fourteenth. How long could it take to get the visa? A few weeks, a month? I figured we would be together again by spring at the latest.

A week later the affidavit arrived. The legal documents looked impressive. The following Tuesday, December 23, I took the train to Rotterdam. It had been snowing since morning, but as soon as the snow hit the cobblestones it turned to slush.

The consulate, a beautiful old brick building, was in the center of town. The receptionist told me the consul had left for his Christmas vacation and would not be back until after the New Year.

"Maybe there is someone else who would help me?" I showed him the affidavit.

"Take a number." He motioned to the cardboard numbers hanging on a nail next to his desk. I sat down with others who were waiting. Now I became aware of the subdued conversation around me. About twenty-five men and women were sitting on chairs and benches. On one wall hung a large map of the United States. I found the black dot that was Los Angeles.

Eventually my number was called. The receptionist took me to a small office. A polite middle-aged man asked me to sit down. My Dutch was poor, my English worse, but the official spoke German. I handed him the affidavit. He gave me a brief, furtive look, and for a moment an expression of compassion appeared on his face.

"The consulate will notify you. There is no need for you to come here personally." I asked him when I could expect my visa. He was noncommittal. The Czech quota was small and oversubscribed.

"Can't you give me some idea, approximately?"

"Sorry, you'll have to wait your turn." The interview was over.

After New Year the consulate sent me a printed form, acknowledging officially the receipt of my affidavit. In February I went to Rotterdam, making another effort to see the consul. He was busy, I was told, and had conferences all day long. Again the clerk promised to let me know as soon as they had an approximate date for a quota number. Walter wrote faithfully every week, trying to raise my sagging morale.

The newspapers were full of Hitler's veiled threats. On March 15, 1939, German troops occupied the rest of Czechoslovakia. In newsreels I could see the Germans marching down Wenceslas Square, the center of Prague. Now there was no way to help my family.

My salary never lasted the entire month. I was paid on the first, but by the twentieth I was usually broke. Then I would visit a pawnbroker in Amsterdam, carrying my mother's fur coat over my arm. The man behind the barred window would offer me 5 guilders—reluctantly. He did not like furs. At due date I would appear with the money to claim the coat, only to show up again a few weeks later to repeat the transaction.

We got to know each other quite well during these months. The coat seemed to grow shabbier every time and so did the old man behind the bars. He would see the coat, shake his head, grumble that he disliked furs because they attracted moths. He would push a claim ticket and the money toward me and I would leave.

Finally the day arrived when he refused the coat.

On the last day of August 1939 I took a weekend off and visited Scheveningen, Holland's most elegant sea resort. I had never seen the ocean. Here was the whole wide expanse of water uncluttered by ships and barges. It was the fashionable world of vacationers, the clean, salt air of the ocean, the kind of atmosphere that filled me with a heightened sense of being alive.

I had left Naarden-Bussum very early in the morning. At the train station in Scheveningen I was given the address of an inexpensive boardinghouse within walking distance of the ocean—exactly what I had hoped for. What I had not anticipated was the lavish breakfast the 1 guilder a night included—meats, eggs, cheese, coffeecake and fruits. After breakfast I quickly changed into my bathing suit, grabbed a towel and ran to the seashore. I threw myself into the ocean, swam out and floated on the crest of the waves. I scanned the string of beautiful hotels facing the beach. On large terraces, people were sitting in wicker chairs. I could hear snatches of music and laughter. Everybody around me seemed alive, and for a wonderful moment I felt free and happy.

On the way back to the boardinghouse—it must have been around lunchtime because the beach suddenly became deserted—I stopped at a newspaper kiosk. There the current attractions were advertised: Maurice Chevalier, guest-starring in a night club, a cabaret troupe performing in the local theater, and then—my heart skipped crazily—the famous tenor Richard Tauber, the great passion of my youth, giving a one-night recital at the Kur Salon. I had 4 guilders left, exactly the price of the cheapest ticket.

Well, I thought ruefully, the concert would be sold out anyhow. Besides, I was suddenly tired and longed for my bed. When I woke up it was late in the afternoon. I decided to go back to the ocean. There I took off my shoes and walked barefoot on the now deserted beach. The first lights in the huge hotels along the coastline had been turned on. In the twilight I noticed the figure of a man approaching. Soon I was close enough to see his face. I stopped. Was it possible?

Was I dreaming? He blinked through a ridiculous monocle and smiled—a somewhat cute, flirty smile. It was my hero, Richard Tauber.

Unlikely as it sounds, I decided that fate itself had maneuvered this meeting on the lonely beach. Somehow I felt that I should take the initiative and talk to him, but I couldn't muster the courage. I just walked past him, my eyes glued to my naked feet. I walked on for quite a while before I stopped and turned my head. He had disappeared. I flopped down—fourteen years old again, a child, filled with longings that did not ask for fulfillment. I was drawing the curtains in my room in Teplitz, cranking up the record player and delicately lowering the needle on the one and only Richard Tauber record I possessed. It was scratchy, worn-down and much misused, but the mellowness, the sweetness, the *schmaltz* of the voice were still there and carried me off into *The Land of Smiles*, the title of a Tauber operetta famous the world over.

Tauber had started his career as a classical tenor. He had always been a star, even as an opera singer. But he achieved his real fame when he appeared in operettas, first in Berlin and later in Vienna. Occasionally he took the leading role in a movie—and I had gone three times to see him in the film version of *The Land of Smiles*.

The price of even the cheapest seat would mean a financial sacrifice; I would have to go without dinner. But to hear Tauber in person seemed worth a little hunger.

An hour before the concert started I stood at the box office window and purchased one of the last available tickets. Soon the concert hall filled, and by curtain time every seat was taken.

I closed my eyes and soaked in the mellifluous voice of the *Meistersinger*. Nothing had changed in the timber of his voice. There was a standing ovation.

Almost automatically I walked out of the hall and toward the stage entrance. I clutched the evening's program. I would do what I had always thought gauche—go backstage and ask for an autograph.

Tauber looked pale and nervous. Gone was his winsome smile. He spoke to everyone politely but somewhat hurriedly. I felt he wanted to get it over with.

Now it was my turn. I told him, stammering slightly, how much I had loved the evening, and asked for his autograph.

"Haven't I seen you before?"

I nodded.

"Oh, yes," he said. "This afternoon—on the beach."

He took the program and signed his name on the cover. "Are you Dutch?"

"No," I said. "I am from Czechoslovakia."

"Ah, Czechoslovakia." He became slightly animated. "From where, Prague?"

"No, Teplitz," I said. "Teplitz-Schönau."

"Teplitz," he said wistfully. "I know it well. I often sang there."

Then he leaned slightly closer, his voice a confidential whisper. "Are you a refugee?"

I nodded.

He smiled. "So am I." He came still closer and the next moment I felt his lips on my cheek. "I wish you all the luck in the world. We all need it."

I walked out of the concert hall. A terrible emptiness invaded me. The feelings of grand passion for a man with a beautiful voice were far in the distant past, and the future held the same perils for both of us.

Looking up, I noticed a cluster of people and heard a high-pitched voice: "Extra edition! Extra edition!!!"

I started running then, knowing instantly that something horrible must have happened. Then I saw the headlines:

HITLER INVADES POLAND

ALL-OUT WAR IMMINENT

Walter

I rented a room within walking distance of the studios. It cost me $3.50 per week. Breakfast was an additional fifteen cents. Dinner (optional) thirty-five cents. My landlord was a retired Navy man, Commander Rock.

At least once a week I saw my family. I was always welcome, or so I was told. Still, I only went there after I had phoned and made certain I was expected.

The worst thing for me was loneliness. I yearned for Hanna. At night I would project silly scenarios onto the ceiling of my room: how I would go back to Europe, marry her, bring her to America, all with the help and—unfortunately—the financial support of my brothers.

I still wrote her often but less than at the beginning. In her letters I began to detect a note of petulance, which I could understand. I felt I had done everything wrong.

Just as I was beginning to feel at home at Columbia, I found a slip in my weekly paycheck envelope informing me my services were terminated. The dreaded pink slip!

Stunned, I left my work and hitchhiked up to Paul's office on Sunset Boulevard. As usual he was busy on several phone lines, but his secretary already knew. Paul had had an argument with Harry Cohn, the Columbia boss. A petty man, he made me the victim.

"Here's some money to tide you over." She handed me a check.

Defeated, I went home. A German hit song of recent vintage turned in my head: "Kleiner Mann, was nun?" (Little Man, What Now?).

However, I found a new job. I became a film projectionist and an entertainer. There was a little movie theater within walking distance of my boardinghouse. They showed silent films exclusively.

A sign in the box-office window read PROJECTIONIST WANTED. Since I had helped run the projector in my father's movie house in Teplitz, I could truthfully say that I was experienced. I was paid $3 a day. When I told the owner that I could also play the piano, he asked me to improvise background music for the second nightly performance (nine to eleven o'clock), while someone else operated the projector.

At eleven I would dash over to Sunset Boulevard and a restaurant called Little Hungary. I played the piano for the late-supper guests. Ten dollars a week and all the goulash I could eat.

I was so excited that I sent Hanna a night letter.

One morning Fritz called me to say that he was driving out to Santa Monica in the afternoon to a kaffeeklatsch at Salka Viertel's. Would I like to come along?

So I would meet the legendary Salka, the friend of Greta Garbo's, a fine actress herself but also a writer and the intellectual hostess of the artistic European emigration.

I became quite apprehensive. Should I really go out there? What would I talk about? What if Thomas Mann should be there (he was said to be a regular) or his brother Heinrich Mann, or other émigré writers such as Bruno Frank, Franz Werfel, Lion Feuchtwanger, and Bertolt Brecht? Should I tell them that I was a film projectionist and piano player? Could I still call myself an actor—with no chance to act?

We arrived at Mabery Road in Santa Monica, parking in front of an unimposing Spanish villa. The day was warm and the guests spilled into the garden.

Salka was a regal woman, with a permanently ironic mien. Her handshake, welcoming me, was warm and genuine. She was sensitive enough to tell Fritz that it was nice of him to bring me along. Among the guests I recognized the German musical star Fritzi Massary; the leading lady of *The Good Earth*, Luise Rainer; the directors Ernst Lubitsch and William Dieterle, the composer Arnold Schoenberg, the actors Alexander Granach and Conrad Veidt. They were all refugees—like me.

It was a typical European party with coffee, tea, strudel and chocolate torte.

Eventually everyone gravitated toward a circular table in a corner of the living room where a large group had formed around a man with sharp features who was speaking French. Fritz whispered to me that it was André Malraux.

It was around five. The sun was slowly dipping into the Pacific below the Viertel home when the front door was thrown open and a young man came storming into the living room. "It's war!" he shouted. "The Germans have just invaded Poland."

Malraux jumped up. Berthold Viertel, Salka's husband, rushed over to the radio in another corner of the room and switched it on. Bulletins reported Hitler's invasion of Poland.

"*C'est le commencement de la deuxième guerre mondiale*," Malraux said.

We all understood. A common terror shook us. For me it was summed up in one thought: What was going to happen to Hanna, my mother and the rest of the family?

The next day Paul made frantic efforts to contact our mother in Teplitz by phone. But he couldn't get a connection. A Teutonic voice seven thousand miles away snarled on the other end that the phone in our home was disconnected and that calls from abroad could only be made to the local Gestapo headquarters.

Reaching it, we were told that the Jewess Kohner would be summoned to their office in twenty-four hours. When Paul finally got through, he listened to our mother's faint, agonized voice begging us to help her to get out of Teplitz.

Paul implored her not to lose courage, telling her that he would do everything humanly possible to bring her to America. Suddenly he was cut off, and when we tried again to get a response, he was told the connection with Teplitz was permanently severed.

In desperation Paul turned to the one man in Hollywood who might be able to help: James Roosevelt. The President's son had taken a fling at producing motion pictures, and he and Paul knew each other professionally. He went to see him in his office. James Roosevelt listened with sympathy and concern to Paul's story of our mother's plight—and jotted down notes on a memo pad. He assured Paul he would do his best. "You'll hear from me," he said.

In Hollywood, this usually meant a polite note of regret—or no reply at all. But twenty-four hours later Roosevelt called Paul. He said that he had spoken to his father and that FDR had given orders to the State Department to get our mother out of Czechoslovakia and to guarantee her safe conduct across the border.

An official of the American consulate in Prague traveled to Teplitz. Outfitted with the proper credentials, he presented himself at Gestapo headquarters. Our mother's Czechoslovakian passport was in order—complete with the entry visa to the United States. All that was needed now was the exit permit from the local authorities. This was given, albeit reluctantly.

There was only one condition: she could take with her only what she wore. Everything else she had to relinquish to the Nazis.

A few days before the arrival of the American official she had buried her heirlooms in the back of our garden. She did it all alone, not even trusting the old gardener who had been almost part of the family. Important as all her other possessions were to her, she gladly turned them over to the authorities. She paid a last visit to the cemetery, filling a small leather pouch with the soil from our father's grave.

The American escort accompanied her first to Munich and then across the Brenner Pass into Italy—and left her side only after he had chaperoned her safely aboard the *Conte Savoia*, which was sailing to New York from Genoa.

A friend of the family welcomed her in New York,

took her to a hotel and put her on a train to California the next day.

Although it was only a year since I had seen my mother, I hardly recognized her. We found her sitting all alone in a compartment of the Super Chief; the train made a brief stop in San Bernardino, where we picked her up. We embraced. She said she was glad to see us, but her words sounded shallow and mechanical. It was as if her sons had become strangers. We got into the big Cadillac and drove her through lemon and orange groves toward Los Angeles. Paul pointed out the landscape, the orchards now in full bloom, the mountain chain slowly descending into the basin of the City of the Angels.

"Wonderful . . . wonderful," our mother repeated dutifully, and then, quite suddenly, she began to cry.

Hanna

I lived in Amsterdam now.

My relatives and I had parted amicably—we were probably all relieved. A small *pension* offered me a new domestic job. Since I spoke German, I could communicate with the boarders, who were well-to-do elderly refugees. I could cook. I was used to heavy work. The pay at the Heinzehuis was just the same as at Cousin Martha's but there were other compensations: I lived in a big city and had opportunities to meet other young people.

I met Irene and Lilo at Huis Oostende. It was a rundown place, donated by a wealthy Jewish family to the Refugee Committee. It became my home on my days off. The Refugee Committee was founded when the first German emigrants arrived in 1933. It was funded by Dutch Jewish sponsors. In the early years the committee provided housing and occasional employment for the refugees. It financed passage for those who were in possession of foreign visas.

I always stopped first at the bulletin board in the vague hope of finding a familiar name, a friend I had lost contact with. It was there that I saw Irene's name and address. She offered English lessons for a small fee. Irene became my teacher and my friend. She was my age (I had just turned twenty), and had moved with her parents from Cologne to Amsterdam in the winter of 1938 to join her brother, Carl, who had been working there for some time. They all were expecting their American visas in the near future.

On a rainy Sunday shortly before Christmas, I went to Huis Oostende. I was about to settle down and do my English work for Irene when I noticed a girl sitting at another table. She was writing, chewing on her pen, her face gnawed by self-doubt. I observed her for a while. What a beautiful girl, I thought. How exquisitely dressed she was. What was she doing there among the shipwrecked?

She must have noticed my inquisitive look and began to giggle. "I have this cousin in America," she said, "and I am trying to explain to him that I haven't got the faintest idea how to pay next month's rent. What would you say?"

"I'd say just what you told me," I said.

"Brilliant idea. Thanks," she said, and continued to write.

A girl like this, I thought, doesn't belong here. Her hair was well-groomed in the pageboy fashion of the time. Her eyes were almond-shaped, and she had beautiful skin, which, though it was winter, seemed evenly tanned.

She suddenly pushed the paper away and turned to me. "To hell with it," she said, smiling brightly. "I'm starving. Can I invite you? Let's go over to the Hotel American."

The American was one of the most elegant places in town. She hasn't got next month's rent, I thought, but she wants to treat me, a complete stranger, to the Hotel American.

That was Lilo.

We went over to the American and she ordered lunch and a bottle of wine. A refugee from Berlin, Lilo was a photographer's model. She had married her husband, Horst, when she was sixteen years old. Both were Jewish, and in 1937 they had emigrated to Holland. Unable to get a work permit, they pinned their hopes on Lilo's American cousin, who had sent them an affidavit. In the meantime their marriage was tottering. Horst, she told me quite frankly, found her boring. He berated her for being messy and unable to hold on to a guilder.

During that winter Lilo and I saw each other frequently. Horst had divorced her by that time—but they remained friends. Once in a while she found work as a model. Occasionally she couldn't pay her rent, and whenever her landlord wanted to evict her, she would persuade him to give her some more time.

I lived for letters. A day without one seemed endless. My parents wrote frequently—and guardedly. Mail from German-occupied countries was censored. They told me that Grandmother Birnbaum had to move to a small single room. She was almost blind.

Walter wrote—not quite as regularly anymore, not quite as affectionately. Around New Year's I got a photo: Walter leaning against a palm tree, smiling. I studied the picture for a long time. After more than a year apart he had almost become a stranger.

Just about this time the American consulate in Rotterdam notified me that a quota number for my visa would not be available before 1942.

* * *

On May 9, 1940—my day off—Irene and I were walking leisurely through Vondelpark toward the inner city of Amsterdam. What a lovely town, I thought. There were flower stands at every corner selling tulips of all shades of the rainbow. We stopped at shop windows to admire the elegant display of spring fashions. I still wore the clothes I had brought from Prague.

"I have some news," Irene said, drawing me close.

"What is it?"

"We got our American visas. My parents have booked passage for the end of June. I will miss you terribly."

I managed a brave smile, telling her how glad I was for her and her family. I was envious.

That evening I had a date with a young man I had met at Huis Oostende. He took me to a sidewalk café. We made some aimless chitchat, talk about the weather and how unseasonably warm it was. It was only May. I didn't like him particularly, but it was better to sit with someone than be alone in an empty room. He took me home, made a clumsy attempt to kiss me, then said something about seeing me again.

Early the next morning I was awakened by frightening noises. I ran to the window, saw low-flying airplanes and heard a distant explosion. The Germans had invaded Holland.

Radio Hilversum gave news bulletins at regular intervals: The Amsterdam harbor had been bombed. Rotterdam was nearly leveled to the ground. There was heavy fighting along the Dutch-German border. Foreigners were restricted to their homes.

Two days later the radio and telephones went dead. By the fifth day it was all over; Holland had surrendered and was occupied by German troops. The royal family fled to England. Many fishermen with seaworthy boats left the Dutch coast loaded with the lucky ones who were at the right place at the right time and who had the money for the journey to freedom—England.

Across the street from the pension stood one of the city's largest hospitals. Day and night, ambulances arrived. We saw stretcher-bearers carrying casualties from the front.

Then the Germans arrived. They occupied all public buildings. Trucks came thundering down the streets, followed by orderly columns of soldiers singing martial tunes. Dutch Nazis (NSBers) made their appearance. Many refugees, who knew what to expect, committed suicide. Entire families ended their lives together.

We were forbidden to listen to Allied radio stations such as the BBC, but people listened anyway. It was our lifeline to freedom. Within a couple of weeks Radio Oranje, the Free Dutch radio station in London, started broadcasting. With a feeling of exultation, we listened to that faraway voice telling us that "things will be better soon," that an underground movement was being organized, that each one of us had to help to defeat the invader.

I was shocked to learn that the American consulate in Rotterdam had burned to the ground. How would I ever get my visa now? Ships were not allowed to leave. Curiously, though, wire services were still func-

tioning. I had a cablegram from Walter. It was wonderful to hear from him, to know he still cared and
worried about me.

I continued with my English lessons. On one of my
Sunday nights off, I went to meet Irene's family.
They lived in an upstairs apartment in a middle-
class neighborhood. When I arrived Irene hugged me
and introduced me to her parents. Her mother embraced me warmly. Her father bowed politely, but
immediately turned away and stared through the
window out onto the street.

The apartment was crammed with all sorts of furniture, mostly antiques. Oriental rugs were rolled up,
ready to be carried away. Boxes containing silverware
and china made it impossible to move about. Irene
explained that the family couldn't make up their
minds whether to keep on packing or begin unpack-
ing. The moving company, hired to load their belongings on a freighter for shipment to America, had never
arrived. Now there was no moving company and no
freighter and maybe no chance for any of them to go
to America.

Dr. Max Benjamin, Irene's father, had been a well-
known pediatrician in Cologne. During the infamous
Kristallnacht in November 1938, he had been arrested by the SS and taken to the concentration camp
of Dachau. That normally would have meant the end,
but one morning, miraculously and without explanation, he was released and permitted to return to
Cologne.

It was, it turned out, his son Carl who had saved
his life. Carl Benjamin! I had heard so much about
him from Irene. He was only twenty-two, but already

a junior executive of an international mining company and working in the main Amsterdam office. Appealing to the company's president, Carl was able to enlist the help of prominent Dutch politicians, who in turn used their power to free Dr. Benjamin and bring the whole family to Holland.

During dinner I observed Irene's father. He looked handsome but frail. He spoke little, and a vacuous smile seemed to be permanently fixed on his face. I could sense how he had suffered, and his sufferings cast a pall over all of us. Only once did he come fully alive—when we heard the noise of the front door being opened.

"That is Carl!" His eyes suddenly flooded with warmth. He got up to embrace his son.

Carl looked mature beyond his years: very tall, slim, with curly brown hair, glasses, hazel-colored eyes and a tentative smile.

Suddenly the climate around the table changed. Carl hadn't eaten yet, and his mother heaped food on his plate. You could feel that he loved the family.

The conversation centered around the German occupation, the war, and what might happen to all of us if Germany was not soon defeated. Carl was far from pessimistic. For all his maturity there was a quality of boyish determination about him.

Around ten Carl offered to take me home. Once in a while we encountered German soldiers, usually in groups, ignoring the civilian passers-by. We walked through the dark streets of Amsterdam, talking about our childhood, our friends, the books and the music we loved. We avoided talking about other commitments we might have made.

When we arrived at my pension we both seemed to want to stay together longer, so we walked up and down the dark street, up and down, until midnight.

We said good night. Carl held my hand for a while, but he made no attempt to find out what I was doing on my next day off.

What a beautiful evening, I thought, climbing up the stairs to my room. And what an attractive man. I felt wonderful. Was I falling in love? Guiltily I sat down and wrote a long, loving letter to Walter.

I waited to hear from Carl. I thought of him all the time. Not since I arrived in Holland had I felt so happy.

Around that time I met a German refugee couple, both actors, both unemployed. With the little money they had managed to salvage, they had started a lending library. Business had been surprisingly good and they needed help. I quit being a maid and became a roving librarian. Every morning I set out on my bike, which I had bought secondhand for 2 guilders, and picked up and delivered books to subscribers, mostly well-to-do refugees who lived in elegant apartments. My salary was meager but I was able to rent a small attic. Though I often went to bed hungry, at least it was my own bed and in my own room.

I prodded Irene to tell me more about Carl. She told me he was very serious, totally devoted to his family. She had given him my new address. Shortly after I had moved in, my landlady yelled up the stairs that I had a visitor. There stood Carl, a bunch of tulips in his hand and a shy grin on his face.

Casually he mentioned that he had two concert tickets
for next Sunday. Would I care to go with him?

He picked me up the following Sunday and we
went to an all-Brahms concert in the Concertgebouw.
I had been in that wonderful old concert hall, whose
orchestra was world-famous, a few times before, but
always up in the gallery. This time we sat downstairs
in the tenth row. I wore my only good dress, of navy-
blue silk, and felt happy and carefree. Silently we
listened. Once in a while Carl touched my hand; we
would look at each other and smile.

By the spring of 1941 the first official anti-Semitic
laws were proclaimed. Already, months before, everyone, whether Jew or non-Jew, had to carry an ID card.

Next to the photograph on the card the letter *J* was
stamped, separating us from the rest of the population. New laws were issued: every Jew had to wear a
yellow star with the word *Jood* written in it. The
star had to be clearly visible on the left side of every
piece of clothing. Even small children had to display
it. Another law banned Jews from all public places,
such as restaurants and theaters. JEWS FORBIDDEN was
painted on park benches. Doctor's offices and hospitals closed their doors to us. Jewish doctors could only
treat Jewish patients. Merchandise in Jewish shops
became scarce. The shopkeepers held back the more
desirable items, to be sold on the black market. Food
became outrageously expensive. I could still afford potatoes, beets and bread. Cigarettes and tobacco became
luxuries, only to be purchased at black-market prices.

From the moment when we started wearing the

star, the reaction of the Dutch was remarkable. Strangers stopped us on the street to shake our hands. They made room for us on public transportation. People we had never met would start conversations about the *Rotmoffen*, a Dutch cuss word for the Germans.

A short time later Jews were forbidden to use the streetcars and railroads. The Nazis dismissed all Jewish musicians from the Concertgebouw orchestra, and prevented Jewish writers from being published and Jewish actors from appearing on the stage.

In at least one unexpected way we profited by these laws. A superb Jewish Orchestra was organized, permitted to play only Jewish composers. In the Schouwburg, a theater in the old ghetto, we enjoyed the music of Mahler, Bizet, Mendelssohn, Saint-Saëns, Offenbach and Dukas. Curfew for Jews was eight o'clock: the orchestra played matinées. For a few short hours we forgot the reality of our lives.

It was now the fall of 1941 and food was beginning to get scarce. Ration cards were distributed. Markets and groceries preferred to sell what little merchandise they had available on the black market for higher prices.

Every Sunday I was invited for dinner at the Benjamins. They would trade silver or linen to buy food on the black market. Every meal was a feast.

Once more I got in touch with my relatives in Naarden-Bussum. They still had their telephone. Jews in Amsterdam were not that lucky. Martha sounded vague.

"How are the children?" I asked her.

"Thanks. Fine. Right now they have colds."

The code among the Jews was that having a cold meant having gone into hiding.

More and more of my friends were joining the underground. The movement had grown since the early days of the occupation. There was no class distinction. People came from all walks of life.

One of my newly acquired friends was Alice, a designer. She, too, was a German refugee. Her great talent was forging ID cards and other documents, and she did it so professionally that no person furnished with her credentials was caught. She moved from Amsterdam to Utrecht. Another underground friend operated a secret radio transmitter that kept him in constant touch with England and the BBC. Others were couriers; others manufactured explosives. Some stole secret Nazi documents; others learned how to kill. Some were caught; some succeeded. But not everyone was a hero. I was afraid to join the underground.

The rental library was still operating but even my small salary was too much for my employer, and he had to let me go. With Carl's help I found a secretarial job with the Joodse Raad, the former Refugee Committee. This was now the umbrella organization for the entire Jewish population of Amsterdam. Soon it came under the jurisdiction of the Germans. They demanded that we keep a file on every Jew living in the city. The registrant had to fill out innumerable documents stating, for instance, which country he would prefer to emigrate to. It was an exercise in sadism, since the registrant—even if he was in possession of a visa—had to apply for a German exit permit, which the authorities never granted. Without one it was impossible to leave Holland. Still more and more forms had to be produced, detailing bank accounts, stocks and real estate. (Another bit of fiendish malevolence; we had long before turned in jewelry and gold coins to Gestapo headquarters.)

I worked in a typing pool of secretaries. Rumors of deportations had been circulating for quite a while. It was said that Jews were being sent to labor camps in Poland, close to the Eastern Front. The same fear of deportation was raised in letters from my family in Prague. I could read between the lines how desperate they were. Naturally all mail was censored. Letters sometimes took as long as two weeks to reach Amsterdam from Prague.

Returning home one evening, I found Lilo waiting for me. We hadn't seen each other for over a year. She still radiated health and beauty, but I noticed a slightly shabby quality to the clothes she wore.

We sat on my bed. I had nothing to offer her, but she took out a package of Lucky Strikes, an unheard-of luxury.

"How is Horst?" I asked her.

"Didn't you hear?" Lilo said.

"What happened?

"He's one of the top men in the underground," Lilo said, "and I work for him." Some of the assignments he had given her sounded like episodes from a bad film. In order to steal some documents she had started an affair with a German officer. While he slept she found the papers in an open drawer—they were important information for the underground. I admired her courage. I could never have done anything like it.

"And how about you and Carl?" Lilo wanted to know. "I heard all about it from Alice. Do you still write to Walter?"

I felt a pang when she mentioned Walter's name. From time to time I had started to write to Walter about what had happened, to tell him there was now another man, a man I was greatly fond of. Deep inside, I knew it was the decent thing to do, to let him know. It was three years now since we had last seen each other. How could he understand the way I lived from day to day, under constant threat, always hungry, not only for food but for human warmth.

Lilo and I talked deep into the evening, and when she left I noted that she was not wearing a star. I went to the window, looked out onto the dark, deserted street.

The attic was cold. The only source of heat was an old electric toaster. I plugged it in, warmed my hands, put on my mother's fur coat, covered the window with the blackout shade, turned on the light and started the letter I knew I had to write to Walter.

Walter

It was May 9, 1940, around eleven at night. Mr. Dora, my boss at the Little Hungary, came over and sat next to me at the piano bench. He told me he had heard over the radio that the Nazis had invaded Holland.

My fingers froze on the keyboard. I got up and asked him if I could use the phone in his office. Not waiting for his answer, I put a call through to Amsterdam. There was of course no connection. The operator told me all lines to Holland were down.

Numb, I went back to the piano and continued playing Viennese waltzes, racking my brain what to do next. The only person I could turn to was my brother Paul. I called him early next morning. He listened sympathetically. But when I asked him whether he could once more appeal to Jimmy Roosevelt to save Hanna, he felt he couldn't impose again on the good will of the President's son. I tried to convince myself that I had done all I could, that I had exhausted all my resources.

I was never far away from a radio, trying to catch every news item about the takeover of the Netherlands. I was haunted by nightmares. I went to the Western Union office and sent Hanna a long, carefully worded cable saying that my thoughts were

with her, telling her how much I loved her and that
I was anxiously waiting for her letters.

More than a year passed. One day I got a call from
my brother Fritz.

"I ran into your former professor," he told me.
"We spoke about you and he mentioned he'd like to
meet you."

I was thrilled. I had never met Max Reinhardt in
person, even though he had been a member of the
Board of Examiners when I was about to graduate
from his school in Vienna in 1937.

Reinhardt was a neighbor of my brother's, and one
Sunday afternoon Fritz took me along to his house.
"So you're Kent?" Reinhardt said, using my European
stage name. I looked around and recognized most of
the guests, among them actors and actresses like Paul
Henreid, Oscar Homolka, Ernst Deutsch, Hedy Lamarr and Marlene Dietrich.

"Your brother told me you are a talented actor,"
Reinhardt said. "I am certain you have some special-
ties on your program." Before I could answer he
walked me over to the center of the patio and clapped
his hands. Everyone looked up.

"Herr Walter Kent, a former student of mine, will
be kind enough to entertain us."

I grabbed a nearby chair just trying to hold on to
something. I told the audience—in German—that I
would give them my impersonation of a street barker
in a small Sudeten German town.

It was something I thought they would appreciate.
Even the sophisticated group of European professionals were not above a good laugh. When I had

finished I saw tears of laughter rolling down Reinhardt's cheeks. Sure of myself now, I gave an encore:
a takeoff on the famous Austrian comedian Hans
Moser.

Before I left, Reinhardt offered me a part in a play
he was going to direct, Pirandello's *Six Characters in
Search of an Author*.

On a muggy autumn afternoon I found myself on
the stage of the Masonic Temple on Hollywood Boulevard (now converted into a theater) with students of
the Max Reinhardt Workshop. Among them were
Nanette Fabray and Robert Ryan. Suddenly I was a
full-fledged member of a group of young actors that
was directed by one of the world's masters of the
theater. My part was a minor one. I was Woody, an
old stage manager, who shuffled from wing to wing
ordering electricians and technicians to light up the
stage. "I want you to fumble around with your watch
on a chain," Reinhardt called out. "Wind it from
time to time." A little nuance, but it added to the
characterization. "No . . . not like that—" Reinhardt
shouted. "Let me show you." He jumped onto the
stage to demonstrate what he wanted. "Let me have
the watch." I handed it to him. Suddenly he was
Woody, a hunched-over, tottering old man. Reinhardt
had an unerring eye for the most trivial detail, an
uncanny ability to impart his concepts to every member of the company.

Opening night was sold out. Thomas Mann, Marlene Dietrich, Gregor Piatigorsky and Bruno Walter
were there as Reinhardt's guests. The evening was a
great success. The rapport between actors and audience was excellent. There was a glow on Reinhardt's

face as he came backstage after the final curtain to congratulate us. I floated a few inches above the ground, almost convinced that my career as an actor was launched again.

On my way home I thought of Hanna. Except for a short letter, I hadn't heard from her for quite some time and I was worried. I had been preoccupied these last weeks with the changes in my own life and had pushed aside my fears for her safety. Reports from Holland and other occupied countries were shattering. A plan to deport all Jews to Polish ghettos had been widely publicized by the Nazis.

The lamp on my bedside table was burning. Propped against it was an air-mail letter. I was happy to see Hanna's handwriting and tore it open. It was a brief letter—just one page.

She wrote that she had fallen in love with another man, a young Jewish refugee from Germany. He loved her. She hoped I would understand. All the wonderful years we had together would always stay with her. She could never forget me, would always love me.

I stared at the letter. It was just a big blur. Was it possible? Of course it was possible. We had been separated for over three years. I had no right to be jealous. Yet the hurt was there when it finally penetrated that I had lost her. I paced my room, then sat down and answered. I knew I would never send that letter.

The next day I walked around in a daze, missing cues at the theater in the second performance. I composed various letters in my mind. It took a few more days before I found the right words. What I said in that letter was that I loved her, as I always had, that I fully understood her need for warmth and protection and hoped and prayed she would not get married. The war would be over one day and we would be together again.

I went to the post office and mailed the letter, then counting the days, waiting for an answer.

Three weeks later there was a letter for me, but this one wasn't Hanna's. It was from the President of the United States sending me greetings.

Shortly after the final curtain had come down on the Pirandello play, I was again on my way to the Masonic Temple, this time for another performance: to be examined by the Hollywood draft board.

The Czech army had rejected me because of my weak eyesight. I expected that the U.S. Army, with its unlimited reservoir of manpower, would certainly send me back to civilian life for the same reason.

Within a week I received a card from the draft board. I had been classified 1A and was to report the following Monday to Fort MacArthur, about fifty miles from Los Angeles. There I was inducted and became Private Walter Kohner, serial number 291675731.

My family gave me a farewell dinner. Afterward I drove my mother home. It wasn't really her home because emotionally she still lived in Teplitz. On the other hand, she made a valiant effort to become part of her new world. She took evening classes to learn the new language so she could communicate with her grandchildren in her broken, and to them, "funny" English. She joined clubs, accepted part-time jobs—all the time fighting the feeling of being uprooted and dislocated.

That evening I watched her climbing slowly up the stairs to her room. She stopped halfway and once more looked at me with a sad, forlorn expression. I quickly turned away, not wanting her to see the tears that suddenly blurred my eyes.

I was sent to Fort Knox, Kentucky, for basic training. On December 7 the Japanese bombed Pearl Harbor. It was only a question of hours before we would be at war officially. Now I was totally cut off from Hanna.

After basic training was over, my company was shipped out. I was the only one left behind. "You're not a citizen," the commanding officer informed me. "They'll transfer you to another place—in the States. Lucky son of a bitch."

I found out that my official file carried the stamp "Security Risk," since I was born in the Sudetenland, now a part of Germany. I pleaded for a hearing. After a thorough investigation of my background, family, friends, education and various other details of my past, I was pronounced trustworthy. Trustworthy, but technically still an enemy alien.

Again I was transferred to another camp, Fort Francis E. Warren, Wyoming, a quartermaster training regiment. Company 1 had just lost a company clerk. I took his place.

One day early in June 1942 Captain Elmo Sheridan, my company commander, came to the orderly room and handed me the daily Cheyenne newspaper. He knew I came from Czechoslovakia. I read the head-line:

CZECH VILLAGE RAZED TO THE GROUND BY THE GERMANS
    Reinhard Heydrich, known as "the hangman of Europe"—head of the SS "Gauleiter" (protector of Bo-hemia and Moravia) was assassinated in Prague, Czechoslovakia, on May 29, 1942. In reprisal the Ger-mans liquidated the small village of Lidice, where one of the assassins was hidden. All the men were executed, women and children deported to Germany. The village was burned to the ground.

Just when I was beginning to feel at home there, my company commander called me to his office. He told me orders had come from G-2 (Military Intelligence) to transfer me to the Stringtown Internment Camp in Oklahoma. "Seems this is a detention camp for German enemy aliens who have been interned for the duration. Someone at G-2 went through the files and found out you speak and write fluent German," Cap-tain Sheridan said. "Obviously they need someone like you in that camp."

On a sweltering August afternoon in 1942 I was the only passenger to get off the train in Stringtown, Oklahoma, population 186.

The commanding officer had sent a jeep and driver to pick me up. We drove for about five miles through flat farm country and cornfields. Stringtown Intern-ment Camp, once a reformatory, stood on a rising slope. Two red-brick buildings and a smaller structure that housed the camp administration were visible be-hind the barbed-wire fence. Outside the compound were a few barracks for the officers and enlisted personnel.

My daily schedule included taking roll call of the inmates in the morning, making out the sick list and censoring incoming and outgoing mail.

The internees represented a cross section of German aliens. They had not received (or even applied for) U.S. citizenship, and for various reasons were considered security risks by the FBI. Among them were farmers, businessmen, a few intellectuals and a doctor. Curiously, there was a group of Samoans, whose islands belonged to the United States. (Before World War I some of the Samoan Islands were a German colony.) They held German citizenship, but didn't speak a word of German and had never been to Germany.

A small group was die-hard Nazis. Even though strictly forbidden, they defiantly and openly displayed swastika buttons in their lapels. When these were confiscated by the MPs, crudely drawn swastikas and paintings of Hitler appeared on the walls of their living quarters. Many, however, were anti-Nazi and there were always conflicts between the two groups.

A typical day at Stringtown Internment Camp started with reveille at six. Breakfast six-thirty. After roll call the inmates were left to themselves. The ones who volunteered were taken by truck to nearby farms to work in the fields; those left behind passed the day by writing letters, playing cards, listening to the radio or doing handicrafts. Dinner was at six-thirty in the evening.

The more affluent internees received packages every week from their relatives or friends. Rudy, who cooked for the inmates, had been a chef in one of New York's finest hotels. He always reserved an extra piece of his famous Bavarian apple pie for me.

One morning a dilapidated, dusty bus drove up to the administration building. A large group of civilians got off. They were German-speaking Jews who had been thrown out of some Latin American country and shipped to the United States in the hope that we would grant them visitor's visas.

Captain McCurtain, the internal security and intelligence officer, asked me to find room for them in the already crowded barracks. I explained to him that the new arrivals were Jewish refugees and could not be put into the same quarters as the Nazis. I warned him of the possible consequences if the two groups were forced to live in close proximity. He didn't seem to understand the difference between a German Jew and a German Nazi. Finally he agreed to call Washington and get clarification. He told me to sit tight and wait for orders. In the meantime, though, I suggested letting the refugees sleep in the camp hospital's unoccupied beds. He agreed—reluctantly.

The refugees looked to me as their protector, their liberator. Most of them did not speak English, and I was besieged with anxious questions. I told them they were safe and should consider themselves lucky to have landed on American soil. They believed me. Orders arrived from Washington the next day to transfer them. They never had to confront the Nazis.

The next morning I accompanied the busload of refugees to the Stringtown railroad station and waved goodbye as the train pulled out.

It was the middle of the day and I decided to pay a visit to Atoka, a small town nearby. I walked along Main Street. A sign read:

WELCOME TO ATOKA
A TOWN UNLIKE ANY OTHER

A man stood in front of the general store. Above the entrance were the words:

B. ROBINS' GRAND EMPORIUM

"Good day, Corporal," he said. "Are you new in town?"

I told him I was stationed at the Stringtown Internment Camp. "Are you Mr. Robins?" I pointed to the store sign.

He nodded. "And you?"

"I'm Corporal Kohner."

He gave me a penetrating look. "Are you . . . perhaps—"

"Yes, I am Jewish," I said, "if that's what you want to know."

A broad smile lit Robins' face. "*Shalom—shalom,*" he said. "Come in, Kohner." He slapped me on the back. "Have a bite to eat. I'll tell the missus."

The Grand Emporium was a country store that carried everything from furniture to hardware to clothing. It was cool indoors and it had a sweet, homey smell that reminded me of a similar store back in a village in Czechoslovakia—one that had belonged to Aunt Toni, a sister of my father's.

From that time on, I was always a welcome guest

at the Robinses. Pearl Robins was a fine cook and I looked forward every week to a tasty meal.

The Robinses had a nineteen-year-old daughter, Deborah, a tall red-headed girl with a small and timid voice. From time to time she helped out in her parents' store. I liked her and she liked me.

We went to the movies together frequently, holding hands, and afterward to the local ice cream parlor. Then I would take her home. There was a swing on the front porch. We set it in motion. Eventually I drew her closer and we kissed. It was a joyless kiss. I knew I didn't love her.

One evening she asked me in her small voice if I had another girl. Maybe back in Los Angeles? I didn't answer. My silence was probably more eloquent than an explanation or confession. When I looked up at her I saw two big tears rolling down her cheeks.

Early in June 1943 the German aliens were transferred to another camp, and the first prisoners of war arrived. They were German navy enlisted men —about fifty of them. We had received advance notice that a number of them were rabid Nazis. In the weeks to follow more and more POWs arrived. Most of them were unwilling to cooperate with the camp routine and complained about everything: the food, the treatment, the slow mail service. Some took offense because they were not allowed to render the "open hand" (Nazi) salute, which, they claimed, they should be permitted to do according to the Geneva Convention.

The truth was that they were treated as well as the German aliens, if not better. They slept in heated dormitories, always had hot water in their showers and ate three well-balanced meals a day prepared by their own cooks. Except for increased security, nothing changed in my daily routine. My duties were still the same, but now I had to face open hostility every morning. The POWs soon found out I was a Jewish refugee. Checking the roster of inmates, I found that they came from all over Germany, including the Sudetenland.

A few anti-Nazis were willing to work on the outside, and despite threats of revenge by rabble-rousers, they went to work on farms in the area. They were paid generously and treated well. Some of the farmers even took them swimming, and on rare occasions to a movie.

In their leisure hours the prisoners could play tennis and soccer, and had at their disposal a library with several hundred English and German books. They built a stage in the gymnasium that served for theatrical performances, and a camp orchestra was organized. The camp canteen was decorated with oil paintings representing German landscapes that had been painted by the POWs. It was a meeting place to buy cigarettes, beer, candies and other items.

Treatment for the sick POWs was provided by the camp hospital, outfitted with the latest modern therapeutic equipment and x-ray machines.

My continuous efforts to speed up my naturalization were finally rewarded. I was notified to appear with two witnesses at the Coalgate Courthouse, the closest district court to Stringown. One of the witnesses was Ben Robins.

Entering the courtroom, I found myself in the company of some fifty townspeople all conversing excitedly in Italian. All of them, the Robinses told me, had lived in surrounding communities since the turn of the century. They were mostly elderly people who had never bothered to take out their first papers. Now that Italy had entered the war against America, they wanted to show their allegiance to their adopted country—their home for so many years.

In alphabetical order we were ordered to face the judge, who questioned us about the Constitution and high points of American history. One of the applicants was an old woman, easily an octogenarian. The judge looked at her kindly, obviously prepared to make it as easy as possible for her.

"Who was the first President?"

The old woman stared blankly at him.

"All right," the judge said, "can you tell me the name of your representative in Congress?"

She shook her head.

"Do you know who has the power to declare war?"

A wide smile spread over the old woman's face and with a voice and an accent barely understandable, she replied, "The enemy, your Honor."

The courtroom roared with laughter.

The judge beamed. "Congratulations. I pronounce you a citizen of the United States of America."

My name was called and I too was sworn in. A few minutes later I received my citizenship papers.

Ben Robins came over and roughly patted my cheeks. "Congratulations, Kohner," he said. "Welcome to the beautiful United States of America!"

A few days later I read an article in the *Stars and*

Stripes, the official Army newspaper. The Pentagon was looking for soldiers qualified in foreign languages. I applied immediately and was accepted at the Military Intelligence Training Center, Camp Ritchie, Maryland.

Hanna

The first roundups started in May 1942. They began with the arrest of young Jewish men on the streets of Amsterdam. Easily identifiable by the yellow stars on their clothing, they were taken away in large trucks. No Dutch citizens were among them; all were refugees. Those caught were supposedly transported to labor camps. No one heard from them again. The Dutch authorities did not object. Rumors of deportations had been circulating for some time. We did not know where they started or who started them. There was talk about Jews being deported to labor camps to help the German war effort. However, we all knew about concentration camps: Dachau, Oranienburg, Mauthausen and Buchenwald. Now a new camp was added: Auschwitz-Birkenau. We knew it was in Poland. It was the official German policy to rid all of Western Europe of its Jews by deportation to Poland.

New decrees were proclaimed daily. One of them stipulated that Jews in important positions were entitled to a special stamp on their ID cards to protect them from being arrested during a raid. As a typist for the Joodse Raad, I became eligible for this privilege. How ridiculous—but, also, how fortunate.

One day in June I was given a list of names and

addresses to be typed. Suddenly my fingers froze to the typewriter—I read the name Carl Benjamin. I tore out the sheet and rushed to my boss's office. I asked him about the list.

"Why do you want to know?"

"Carl, my boyfriend, his name is on the list."

My boss got up, walked over to the door and closed it. "What I am going to tell you is strictly confidential," he said, almost in a whisper. "There is a possibility that this is a list of people who may be deported to a labor camp." When I asked if there was anything I could do to protect Carl, my boss shrugged his shoulders. It was that helpless shrug I was to see so often in the weeks to come.

"How about the stamp on my ID card? Will that protect me?"

"As of now it will—probably."

It was always "probably."

"If I had a husband, would he also be protected?"

"Probably," he added, with another shrug.

My boss understood that typing deportation lists was unbearable for me. He was a decent and kind man and held on to his position in the so-called Emigration Department to protect himself and his family.

That evening I asked Carl to marry me as soon as possible. I was fully aware that it might merely postpone the inevitable. So far, only young single men had been arrested and deported, which made Germany's claim of sending them off to labor camps seem plausible.

Carl agreed. We both had been very sure of our love for each other, hoping against all reality for a quick German defeat and the return of normal times.

We were both so young—I twenty-two, Carl twenty-three—and had dreams of a wedding with my family present, a life with a home and children.

I wrote to my parents of my forthcoming marriage. "You seem to be very happy," my mother wrote. "That makes all of us here happy, too. We cherish the photo you sent us. Carl looks like the kind of man I would have wished for you."

Then came the nerve-racking process of obtaining a marriage license. The bureaucratic obstructions were unbelievable. Couples under the age of twenty-five had to bring a notarized letter from their respective parents approving the marriage. Once the letter was received, the files were checked for any possible criminal record. Every visit to City Hall meant a long walk into downtown Amsterdam. We were not permitted to use streetcars or buses any longer, and months before had been forced to turn in our bicycles. We stood for hours in anterooms waiting for our turn. Because of the long trip home, where we had to be before the eight o'clock curfew, we sometimes had to leave without accomplishing anything.

Every night in my room I listened to the footsteps outside, praying that the heavy-booted ones would pass. Friends of ours had lately been picked up in night raids. The SS would block a street on both ends and systematically check each apartment for Jews, sometimes arresting them, sometimes leaving them, in a completely haphazard way.

Before America entered the war, I had received one more letter from Walter. I decided not to answer anymore; I had said all that needed to be said. When I saw his handwriting I still felt a bittersweet pain of love and memories. Memories that belonged to a different person in another world.

On July 30, 1942, Carl and I were married. There were actually two ceremonies. The first one was at City Hall, followed by a religious one in an Orthodox synagogue. The only temple left in Amsterdam was miles away from where we lived, so we had to start out early in the morning. It was a long walk.

Carl's parents had given us an upstairs room in their apartment. From now on we all lived together. My mother-in-law had sewn my white wedding gown. On it the yellow star looked grotesque. A friend had contributed an exquisite veil. On our way, we were cheered by passers-by. Many Jewish couples were getting married. With deportation threatening everyone, all that mattered was the hope of at least being together—wherever the Germans would send us. At City Hall twenty-five couples said their vows that morning.

The Orthodox rabbi in the ghetto synagogue refused to perform the ceremony without gold rings. But we had long ago turned in all our jewelry to Gestapo headquarters and were strictly forbidden to own or buy any gold. The rabbi had faced this situation before. He offered us his own wedding ring, lending it to Carl for the ceremony.

My in-laws had made arrangements for a modest wedding breakfast in the only remaining Jewish restaurant. It cost us our ration stamps for one week, which went for some rolls and cheese, but they tasted heavenly. Surrounded by friends and Carl's family, I felt, for the moment, happy.

Carl still had his job. It had become pro forma

work only. A German *Verwalter*—an Aryan manager—had been installed at the firm. Since the majority of the company's ore mines were located outside Germany, and since most of its capital was de-
posited in foreign countries, there was little business
conducted. Nevertheless, two senior directors and the
remaining employees went to the office each day. The
German manager was a fairly decent man. It was in
his own interest to keep the place going.

Dr. Benjamin, like all other refugee doctors, had
never been permitted to practice in Holland and
found little to fill his days. My mother-in-law—an
expert seamstress—made dresses at home for acquaintances who were still fortunate enough to be able to
buy some fabrics. Irene at one time wanted to study
medicine. She now had taken a course in midwifery.
The little money we all earned kept our household
going.

Then, late one evening, six weeks after our wedding, footsteps stopped in front of the Benjamin apartment. The bell rang. We looked at each other. Dr.
Benjamin opened the door. Two Marrychausses
(Dutch policemen) and two SS men stood in the
hallway.

"Hanna Bloch?"

I stepped forward, showing my stamp on the ID
card and explained that I was now legally married
to Carl Benjamin. Bloch or Benjamin, they had orders
to take me along to headquarters. All former Czech
citizens were being rounded up. The Germans usually
worked by lists, of which they had many. Sometimes
by nationality, as in my case, or alphabetically or by

age or by marital status. They even had sick lists. Once they emptied the entire Jewish hospital. The SS occasionally decided on a raid, called a *Razzia*. Jews were taken at random, either off the street or out of their homes.

Carl asked for permission to accompany me. There must have been a mistake—he could easily straighten everything out. We picked up our knapsacks on the way out.

There were knapsacks ready in every Jewish household. Each member of the family had packed the most essential belongings: warm clothing, medicine, toilet articles, sturdy shoes or boots, and a tightly rolled blanket. I also had with me photographs of my parents, my brother and grandmother.

Many times in the past we had discussed the possibility of going into hiding. The underground supplied names of Dutch families who would hide Jews— some for humanitarian reasons, some for financial gain. Food was a problem. Since fugitives had no ration cards, the people who hid them had to buy provisions on the black market. They risked their lives and those of their families, as there was constant danger of being caught. Carl's father fiercely opposed any plan to go into hiding. Most of the Dutch were genuinely helpful, even heroic. But there were also traitors. Once caught, people were sent on a *Straftransport* (penal transport). As a rule, these transports went directly to concentration camps.

The SS had requisitioned for its headquarters a large modern school in Amsterdam's most elegant district, Amsterdam-Zuid. Day and night people living nearby heard screams coming from the building. They knew all too well what was happening behind the thick walls of the Euterpestraat school.

We were taken to the gym; it was crowded with hundreds of Jews, many of them Czech citizens. All through the evening new prisoners were brought in, among them some of our friends who also had stamps like mine on their ID cards.

Carl and I spotted the SS commandant and approached him. Carl explained to him that we had just gotten married, told him where he worked, and said that I had a stamp in my ID card because I did important work at the Joodse Raad.

A grin spread over the man's face. "You should not leave your wife alone," he said. "Perhaps you had better go with her."

Now Carl was hopelessly trapped. Tears came to my eyes; I reached out for his hand and pressed it. He turned his face to me and smiled.

After hours of waiting we were herded onto trucks and driven to the Schouwburg theater in the old ghetto, where only a year before we had enjoyed our Sunday concerts. Now it was a collection center for transports.

Invalids were taken to the loges, where a temporary sickroom had been set up. All windows and exit doors had been closed and darkened against possible air raids: the smell and the wailing were intolerable.

Hours later we were again herded into trucks and driven to the railroad station.

Camp Westerbork, where we were taken, had been built before the war to house illegal Jewish immi-

grants caught by Dutch border patrols. The government of Holland was at that time well aware of the
plight of these people and did not intend to deport
them. Afraid they might become a public burden, it
sequestered them in a deserted area eighty miles east
of Amsterdam. About three hundred refugees lived
there in barracks. Financially supported by the Joodse
Raad, they were waiting to go to Palestine or to any
country that would grant them a visa. The inmates
were permitted to have visitors and occasionally even
got passes to travel to Amsterdam. The situation
changed, however, once the Germans occupied Holland. The camp became the first stop for the Jewish
deportations.

After hours of being locked up in a commuter train,
we came to a final stop at a little station. Daylight
broke. We took our knapsacks and started moving. A
line formed. Carl and I held hands. We walked
through the blooming heather. The sweet smell of
flowers was everywhere. Birds were twittering.

Camp Westerbork appeared out of the flat landscape. First we saw the high barbed-wire fences, then
four towers manned by SS sentries. Machine guns
were pointed at us.

Under the eyes of an SS man, we were ordered to
empty our pockets, turn over our ID cards and whatever money we had. Then we were sent to the showers to be checked for lice. Finally we were dispatched
to our barracks. I offered a silent prayer that I would
find Carl—and there he was, waving at me. We were
so happy to be together that we couldn't speak; we
just clung to each other.

Our barracks—it was one of the smaller ones—

housed about a hundred people; it was divided in the center. One side for women, the other for men. This was solely a sleeping arrangement; during the day and especially at mealtime we could visit either side.

Next to each three-decker bunk stood a wooden table and benches. The washroom was located in the rear, with rows of latrines and cold-water faucets. Inside the barracks it was noisy and dusty. I picked an upper bunk, threw down my knapsack onto it and went with Carl to look at the rest of the camp.

Soon we discovered the inconsistencies of camp life. There were the "old" barracks where the "settlers" of the camp lived; Westerbork had been home for some since 1938. The buildings were clean and resembled prefabricated apartments. Many had miniature gardens with vegetables and flower beds. Behind the windows hung ruffled curtains. The settlers were bitter men and women, who reminded us constantly how fortunate we had been to have lived in freedom all these years. Under SS supervision, they ran the camp, the hospital, the kitchen and the warehouse, where food and other necessary provisions were stored. They also had the important position as barracks leaders and were in charge of the administration and the crucial assignment of compiling lists for deportations out of Westerbork.

Most of the Jews who had been picked up in Holland came through Westerbork on their way to Eastern Europe. Some were fortunate enough to remain there for a while. Connections with the leaders of the camp helped. At times the Joodse Raad intervened for certain individuals. Doctors were always needed and had a good chance of staying; nobody cared in which country they got their degree.

We were allowed to walk about the camp freely. Next to the central administration building were the bathhouse, the camp kitchen, the laundry, the hospital, a post office and even a library.

Carl was assigned to the scrap-iron yard. I worked in the hospital post office, a small shed in the hospital compound. We were permitted to write one letter a week and could receive mail—even packages. All this was under strict censorship.

At noon a whistle blew. Work stopped. Everyone went back to the barracks for the only hot meal of the day, a souplike stew of beets, potatoes and dried vegetables. Inmates who worked in the kitchen stole most of the better ingredients. Only small portions of vile-tasting food were left for us. Carl and I were able to supplement our rations with packages sent by my in-laws.

The hospital was actually a complex of barracks. It was run by a German-Jewish surgeon who had been a passenger on the ill-fated ocean liner *St. Louis*, the refugee ship that couldn't find a port in the New World. The ship had to return to Europe. The doctor was a tired-looking middle-aged man who had a weakness for pretty young girls. The outpatient clinic was headed by an old Jewish doctor. He had a number of assistant doctors working under him, as well as nurses, lab technicians and orderlies.

Every morning I would sort out mail and parcels for the patients and deliver them. The largest barracks was the TB ward. Most of the patients in it were

terminal cases. Then there was the orphanage, full
to bursting with children of all ages. Although some
actually came from a Jewish orphanage raided by the
Nazis, others were children discovered by the SS in
hiding places. Some had come to Westerbork with
their parents, who had later been deported to the east.
With the help of the inmates working at the administration, they had left their children at Westerbork
in the hope that their lives would be spared.

Routinely the SS demanded a certain number of
persons to be sent on a transport east. Camp leaders
working on transport lists replaced the children's
names with those of adults.

Anybody who was not too old or sick had to work.
Many assignments were absurd: sorting out old dead
batteries, cutting turf that was never used; making
stuffed dolls of scrap materials to be sold outside
the camp. No one complained. We knew that things
were tolerable as long as we could stay on Dutch soil.

We rarely had personal contact with the SS. The
only ones we saw were stationed on top of the watchtowers and those who supervised incoming and outgoing transports.

The commandant of Camp Westerbork was a young,
good-looking, elegantly dressed German officer. From
time to time he went on an inspection tour of his
domain, usually wearing civilian clothes. He looked
more like the leading man in an English stage play
than an SS Hauptsturmführer.

A few weeks after our arrival in camp, new barracks were being built. Everyone assumed that more
incoming transports could be expected soon. The fall
weather was cold. There were rumors that other trans-

ports would be leaving the camp for unknown destinations.

On the morning of December 2, 1942, Carl was called to the commandant's office. It was a terrifying moment. When he returned he was beaming. The commandant had received an order from Amsterdam's SS headquarters to release Carl and send him back to Amsterdam. We couldn't believe it. The German director who now headed the company where Carl had been employed had requested his return. It was an unusual demand, but the man obviously had influence. There was no indication, however, that I, too, would be released.

The following day a runner, one of the young boys who worked as messengers between SS headquarters and the inmates, appeared in our barracks. Carl's hands shook as he took the sealed envelope the boy handed him. He asked me to open it. Both of our ID cards were attached to a note ordering us to pick up our travel permits and train tickets the next morning at six. I handed the note to Carl. He read it again, carefully. We looked at each other. Our eyes were wet.

Word that we were to be permitted to leave spread quickly. Everyone in our barracks was happy for our good fortune. If it was possible for us, it might be possible for others. Suddenly there were smiling faces. Friends came around to give us messages for those on the outside.

Shortly before six in the morning we stood in front of an SS man at the closed gate. It was still dark. He examined our permit, handed it back to us, and gave another SS man the sign to open the gate.

Holding hands, not daring to speak, we walked along the path to the railroad station. We kept turning around, expecting any minute for someone to yell at us to stop, or even worse—to shoot at us from the towers.

When we arrived at the station it was ten minutes after six. The commuter train came puffing in. We boarded quickly. We sat down and looked at the passengers. Everybody in the car tried hard to ignore us. They probably couldn't figure out how two Jews could be getting out of Westerbork and taking a train to Amsterdam. Eveyone living in the vicinity was familiar with the camp and its purpose.

I have known many moments of happiness, and one of them was getting off the train at Amsterdam's railroad station. We stepped out—free to move, unguarded, just wearing the telltale badge on our clothes.

Carl's parents had written that they had been forced to move into the Amsterdam ghetto. We had the address. Dusk fell when we arrived in the old section of town with its rows of tenement buildings. The whole day they had been waiting for us. After we finally arrived, after everyone had hugged everyone, we looked around. The new place was tiny and shabby. But to Carl and me it was heaven. We didn't mind the improvised kitchen and the one toilet for the whole floor. We didn't mind anything. We were free.

Carl's mother had sold some of her exquisite table linen to buy meat on the black market for our homecoming feast.

It was wonderful to see Irene again. She told me of a young man she had recently met. He would come the next day to visit. Obviously she was anxious for our approval. Because of her work as a midwife, she was now in possession of a stamp on her ID card. But we all knew how little that meant.

The next morning Carl went back to his old office, and I set out to visit the Joodse Raad. My boss was still in charge of the ever-growing Jewish organization, and he offered me my job back. I was delighted— even though many of my old coworkers and colleagues had disappeared. Some had gone underground; some had been deported.

Carl kept busy with paperwork in his office, most of it useless. The German manager had saved him for a job that for any practical purposes was nonexistent. We were fully aware that our situation was tenuous. The only hope was a speedy defeat of Germany.

Once in a great while an incident, such as our release from camp, lifted everyone's morale. The general feeling in the Jewish community tended to be optimistic, particularly since America had entered the war. If we could hold out a little longer, another week, another month, another year, the Germans would be beaten. Many times I thought of Walter. I wondered if he was now a soldier in the American army. Whatever he was doing, I wished him well.

The winter of 1943 was rough. We suffered. The old Joodenbuurt—the Jewish neighborhood, which had become the ghetto—was an area of about twenty square blocks. There were no visible walls surrounding it, but now only Jews were living in this district.

Curfew for us was eight o'clock. Any footsteps heard in our neighborhood after that hour could only mean disaster.

The weather had turned very cold. There was one small stove in our apartment. Coal was rationed, but often it was not available even with ration stamps. Food was scarce, bread a luxury. We ate potatoes for breakfast, at noon and for dinner. At times we would be able to buy some beets that ordinarily were used as pig fodder. Whatever else we needed had to be bought on the black market. My mother-in-law was enormously resourceful in selling and trading her linen, china and crystal—items the Gestapo had not yet confiscated.

With five people in two rooms anything resembling a harmonious family life became difficult. My father-in-law still suffered from severe depression. From time to time he threatened to turn on the gas in the kitchen and bring an end to our misery. He was a fine, decent man, but he had reached the breaking point. We never dared to leave him alone, even for a moment.

Spring came, and somehow life seemed easier when the sun appeared.

We had learned to read the German-controlled newspapers between the lines. When we read of "victorious redeployment" on various battlefields, we knew the opposite was true. Our eyes were finely tuned, and so were our ears. We learned to distinguish between the sounds of German and Allied planes. At night we listened to the constant roar of engines. When we heard hundreds of planes flying overhead, we knew that Germany would be bombed again that night. It was music to us.

Some Sunday afternoons we would get together with old friends, among them Coen and Magda. Coen (in Dutch, short for Conrad) was a psychiatrist; his wife, Magda, originally came from Prague. They carried forged documents and were still living in their own house in one of Amsterdam's fashionable districts. The Germans did not suspect that they were Jewish. Their house had become one of the centers for the underground. We would usually discuss the political situation and the rumors that circulated. Often we listened to the few records we had been able to save. We all looked forward to our next get-together, planned for June 16.

On that beautiful morning we were awakened by the noises of large military trucks in the street below. We ran to the window. A loud chilling voice came over the bullhorn. "Jews—Jews." I turned to Carl. All color had drained from his face.

"A *Razzia*," he said.

All Jews were ordered to come out of their houses with their luggage and assemble at the nearby square to await further instructions. There was no way out. The roads were blocked in all directions. Wordlessly we packed whatever food was in the house.

The bullhorn voice outside stopped. An eerie calm settled. I looked at the stack of old records including the Schumann piano concerto I had prepared the previous night for our gathering. From my night table I took the book I had been reading, Hemingway's *The Sun Also Rises*.

I reached for the photo of my parents, wondering whether I would ever be able to write to them again. The closet door stood open. My mother's fur coat seemed to say goodbye to me. The cuffs were worn thin and the collar had acquired a greenish sheen.

Who would find the coat, who would wear it? And not without a touch of cynicism, I thought, the coat might have a longer lifespan than I.

We all left the apartment together. I stole a look at my father-in-law; the face of that gentle man suddenly showed amazing strength and calm. His voice was steady and reassuring. He led us down the stairway to the street.

People converged from all sides. Policemen shouted at us to walk faster. On the square at the end of the street, empty streetcars and large military trucks were waiting. We were pushed into one of the streetcars. A German shepherd was tied to a lamppost. Obviously abandoned, he cried woefully for his master. One by one the cars started to move in the direction of the railroad station. The whole area was cordoned off. We realized that by now neither a stamp in the ID card nor Carl's position would any longer be of help.

We arrived at Westerbork in the early morning of the following day. The tracks now led directly into the camp. Many new barracks had been built. The routine of being deloused and registered was still the same, only many more new arrivals were being processed.

We ended up in one of the newly built barracks—Number 68, again women in one half, men in the other. The new barracks were as bleak as the old ones, only bigger. We found so many friends from our first stay in Westerbork that our reunion had almost a holiday atmosphere. It did not last long. Already there were rumors that we soon would be on a transport to other camps—Auschwitz, Theresienstadt, Bergen-Belsen.

We had known about these camps for a long time. It is difficult to tell who mentioned them first. Details were sketchy, but the rumors about these places were horrifying. In Westerbork a friend of mine told me about gas chambers in Auschwitz. I could not believe him, and said so. He immediately regretted having disclosed this secret, which, if it got back to our captors, could be fatal for him. This same friend, I found out much later, was a member of the underground. One night, after a transport had just arrived in Westerbork and the empty train was returning to Amsterdam, he, with the help of a few others, doped a dozen children from the orphanage, tied them securely to the underside of one of the boxcars and smuggled them out of the camp. They were rescued in Amsterdam by other members of the underground and shipped all the way to Palestine.

My father-in-law was now a doctor in the camp hospital, where his wife and Irene worked as nurses. Carl was back in the scrap-iron yard, and I was assigned to work for the Joodse Raad, registering new arrivals. In the months that followed, trainloads of Jews came from all over Holland, from every Dutch city, town and hamlet.

A week in Westerbork had six days: from Tuesday noon until Monday morning, when the train with empty cattle cars arrived. Sometimes in the middle of Sunday night we would hear the sound of the train whistle and shiver in our beds.

On Monday night, lists with the names of inmates to be deported were posted in the barracks. The doors were locked. There were no farewells, no last embraces—it had to happen, sooner or later. On Tuesday morning the train, usually ten to twelve cattle cars, was filled. There were old people, young people, babies. Those too sick to walk were carried on stretchers; a dubious load for labor camps. At times the SS specified who had to be on a transport. They would, for instance, insist on fifty patients from the hospital or families with small children; the Jewish camp leaders then had to make the final selection.

The same elegant SS commandant was still in charge. He and his officers in immaculate black uniforms stood on the platform of the station supervising the transport. After the train had left we would go from barracks to barracks to see who had been spared.

Among the prisoners in Westerbork were many distinguished actors, writers and musicians, all refugees caught by the invading Germans. The SS commandant decided to use their talents for a cabaret evening. Costumes were ordered from Amsterdam, and a stage was built. Two pianos arrived. On Saturday all was ready for the performance.

The first row was reserved for SS officers and their guests. Camp inmates made up the rest of the audience. At eight o'clock the curtain went up. The actors gave an extraordinary performance. For many it was their last. Those cabaret evenings were the only break in the monotony of the weeks and months that followed. People got used to a certain routine; there was almost something normal about it. Babies were born, romances bloomed, couples split up. Children went to school in makeshift barracks. Meanwhile, we continued to wait for the dreaded Tuesday. When children did not show up for a class, we knew what had happened. When teachers weren't in classrooms, new volunteers took over. One Tuesday nearly half of the orphanage was emptied. The children, all neatly dressed, and most of them too young to understand what was happening, were loaded on the train. Some of the orphanage nurses volunteered to accompany them.

Then, on a drizzly morning, a trainload of "special prisoners" arrived. They were Jews who had gone underground and had been caught in their hiding places. Stripped of all their belongings, they were given blue prisoner's garb with a large red letter *S* on their backs, meaning *Strafstransport* (penal transport). This contingent didn't go through the normal routine of registration. We knew that their stay in Westerbork was only a brief stopover. That evening I was handed a note by my barracks leader:

Dear Hanna,

I have heard you were here. For obvious reasons I could not get in touch with you. We were caught on a train to Switzerland. We had false passports—bought from people who were supposedly trustworthy. It was all a trap. There might not be much time left for all of us, so I wanted to let you know how guilty I have felt all these years that I had no better understanding for you. Please forgive me.

Martha

I tried everything to obtain a permit to visit with my cousin, but the next day the entire barracks for the "special prisoners" was empty. Later in the winter of 1943–1944 another transport arrived. All of them were Gypsies. They had often come through Teplitz, mostly in the spring, with children shouting and laughing and laundry hanging out the windows of their garish, horse-drawn wagons. Women would grab the palm of your hand and tell you your fortune. Their earrings tinkling, they promised you a long and happy life. Now they were here, on a hard winter day, looking grotesquely alien and outlandish in the sober flatlands of Holland, the laughter gone. Looking petrified, they were herded into the delousing barracks, and after a while appeared again, wearing white turbans, a sign that they had indeed had lice and that their hair had been cut. They were quarantined in the *Strafbaracke* till the following Tuesday.

The *Strafbaracke* (penal barracks) was used for special prisoners only—Jews who had been caught in hiding, or in this case the Gypsies. That barracks was encircled by barbed wire and was located in the farthest corner of the camp, a prison inside a prison.

The next morning I looked out of the window and saw a long, dark, silent line moving toward the train. At the head were the Gypsy king and queen, a regally calm expression on their faces. Not a sound was heard, not a word was spoken, not a child cried. And then they were gone.

In Westerbork people were not killed; they died of disease, or from hunger, and from misery. Our commandant apparently did not want to dirty his hands with murder. He did it indirectly. Anybody he wanted to get rid of he sent on a transport to Auschwitz.

Alfred was Carl's best friend. They had gone to school together in Cologne. He was best man at our wedding. He had been in Westerbork for two weeks; one day he decided to try to break out. As far as we knew, no one ever had succeeded in escaping; Alfred, too, was caught. As punishment he was put on top of the watchtower with the SS, and there had to stand day and night, his hands and feet tied.

The following Tuesday, Alfred was gone.

A hand-printed postcard arrived (all camp mail had to be printed, so it could easily be censored) and I could feel my heart speed up. The card was from my parents and Friedl. They were alive—in Theresienstadt.

Theresienstadt, a small garrison town in Czechoslovakia, about seventy miles from Prague, served as a transit camp for Jewish prisoners from Germany and all German-occupied countries. From there, we learned, transports went to Auschwitz and other concentration camps.

My parents were permitted to write this one last card before leaving for Auschwitz. We had heard of the horrors of that place. How could they possibly survive there?

The stinging cold of the winter had set in. The barracks were freezing. Food was scarce and inedible. The miraculous event of that winter was the arrival of a package. It came from Carl's Aunt Betty in Sweden—the only Scandinavian country not occupied by the Germans. We had been in contact with Aunt

Betty as long as we had lived in Amsterdam, and at one time she had asked for a passport photo from each of us, promising to do everything in her power to get us entry visas into Sweden.

On top of the food package were five Ecuadorian passports. We had become citizens of Ecuador. We were jubilant. Immediately we went to work, hoping to get transferred into one of the internment camps for foreigners.

The camp officials told us that others had similar documents but had been turned down. Many inmates had Palestinian certificates which might help them to be sent to internment camps or eventually to be exchanged for Germans in enemy hands. It was a pipe dream. Still, we held on to those precious documents. Maybe one day the authorities would change their minds.

Chanukah, the festival of light, goes back to the time when the Jews defeated the Syrian tyrant Antiochus. After cleansing the temple in Jerusalem of Syrian idols, they found only one small remaining container of oil for the holy lamps, just enough for one day. Miraculously, the oil lasted for eight days. Each day of Chanukah ever since, one more candle is lit, until on the eighth day all candles in the menorah are burning. This holiday falls around the time of Christmas. It was Chanukah 1943; we lit the first candle.

The following day came an order from the commandant: no festivities of any kind, nor any candles, were allowed. As darkness fell, a short-circuit blacked out the entire camp, including the watchtowers and

SS quarters. To prevent breakouts in the dark, candles were distributed in all barracks. We had our own little miracle, and our second night of Chanukah.

With the new year came further restrictions: we could no longer receive mail or packages. The last transport from Amsterdam brought Holland's chief rabbi and his large family. His youngest son, Bram, was quartered in our barracks, and we became friends. Bram was a gentle, sweet young man. His best friends were Jo and Jo's wife, Rosie. They, too, had their bunks in our barracks. Jo was a professional cantor with an angelic voice. On Sunday afternoons, while we sat hungry and freezing around the table, Jo would sing for us. He had brought along his music books, and sang songs by Schubert, Brahms and Schumann.

Jo, Rosie and Bram were Orthodox Jews. Friday was the only day when pieces of meat (of questionable origin) appeared in the watery soup. No matter how hungry our friends were, they would not touch the soup. Every Friday they went without food.

On a Monday night at the end of January 1944, the weekly list was posted in our barracks. Jo's and Rosie's names were on it. So close had we become in our short friendship that I almost felt it was Carl and I who had received the verdict.

I helped Rosie pack. We traded clothes. I gave her some of my warm underwear. She insisted that I take her silk blouse embroidered with red flowers. After we finished packing, we sat on her bunk and held hands; Rosie confided to me that she was pregnant. Jo was the only one who knew. I felt deeply touched by her trust in me. Bram's name was not on the list, since he and his family had Palestinian certificates and there was still talk about prisoner exchanges between Germany and England.

Shortly after the departure of our friends a regular train arrived in camp. It was announced that all prisoners with Palestinian papers or foreign passports were to be taken to Bergen-Belsen. No one was forced to go—it was a "voluntary" transport. Dr. and Mrs. Benjamin and Irene decided to go. Carl and I chose to stay in Westerbork. Our response was purely emotional because we still clung to the hope that we could stay there until the end of the war. And that would be, we thought foolishly, any day now!

The one thing in Westerbork that almost pushed me to the breaking point was the utter lack of privacy. Fleas, hunger and cold were bad enough, but the constant presence of other people was unbearable. I never came to terms with it. We, like everyone else in our barracks, envied the few lucky ones who had their own room with a door to close.

After the large transport for Bergen-Belsen had left, the camp population shrank visibly. No new trains arrived for weeks. Thanks to some influential friends in the administration Carl and I were given a room all to ourselves. It had two iron beds and a wooden crate that served as a table and a chair. The front room, larger than ours, was occupied by a middle-aged couple and their two daughters. They were kind, quiet and polite. Eva, the older of the girls, became my friend.

One day there was a train. It stood locked up on the tracks for two days. Slowly the news filtered out:

the human cargo was the nurses and inmates of the Dutch insane asylum of Apeldoorn. Members of our hospital staff brought them water and food. Then the train left.

And then there were the two fliers shot down over the camp. They were Americans. Their white parachutes floated right into the center of the camp. We all stared transfixed. They were angels, bringing good tidings. We felt like shouting, but were afraid of the guards.

Curfew was called immediately. Word was passed swiftly that the Americans were alive and had only sustained minor injuries. Next day they were transferred to a POW camp. Our surgeon, who had taken care of them, proudly wore a beautiful fur-lined leather jacket, a gift from one of the American flyers.

In June 1944 some prisoners who worked for the SS outside the camp returned with new rumors. The Allies had invaded Europe. They had no idea where or how, but they had overheard some men discussing it. It was too good to believe!

At times the night sky was lit up by the glare of distant fires. The port of Emden was supposedly burning. The roar of planes was heard almost nightly.

At the end of summer one more big transport from the provinces arrived in Westerbork. I was sitting at my typewriter recording the names and dates of the new arrivals when a voice called out: "Hanna—I knew I'd find you here!"

I looked up and there stood my old friend from Amsterdam, Lilo. We embraced, shed a few tears and then laughed. She wore a spotless, elegant white suit, a silk blouse and high-heeled pumps. A lovely straw hat with a bunch of violets completed her outfit. Instead of the obligatory knapsack, she carried a yellow leather suitcase. Only now did I notice the tall, attractive man standing next to her, also immaculately dressed, smiling self-assuredly.

"Hanna, meet Michael," Lilo said, her politeness in no way tarnished by the unlikely surroundings. "We've been married a year. I never had a chance to let you know—"

Michael bowed and kissed my hand. "I'm glad to meet you, Hanna," he said. I had seen him somewhere before. His face was vaguely familiar—and then I knew. He was a Dutch opera singer I had heard years ago in *Madame Butterfly*.

"Lieutenant Pinkerton, I presume?" I said.

A broad smile spread over his face.

The next morning they were gone.

Toward the end of summer we received orders to tear down the big barracks now standing empty. It seemed the Germans had succeeded in deporting all the Jews in Holland.

One empty cattle train arrived—but it didn't leave. It stood there at the entrance to Westerbork.

About two thousand inmates were left in the camp. There was speculation whether the entire camp would be liquidated, or maybe only half of it. So far Carl and I had been unbelievably fortunate; but we knew that if there was another transport, our connections with camp leaders would not help us any longer.

On September 1, 1944, I went to the hospital; the doctor confirmed I was pregnant. I had known it for

a while, and Carl and I had agreed that I should have
an abortion. It was of course illegal and the doctor—
afraid of possible consequences—refused to help.

On September 3 the doors to the cattle cars were
unlocked. Our time had finally come.

The commandant and his staff stood as always on
the platform supervising the transport. Impatiently
hitting his shiny black boots with his riding crop, he
watched our departure. Another SS man checked the
names from a list. The transport of about eight hundred people went according to plan. The doors were
locked.

We were each given a slice of bread; one large garbage can for each car served as a toilet. The camp
leaders had been informed by the SS that our transport was going to Theresienstadt in Czechoslovakia.
My first thought was of my parents. Might they still
be there?

A trip that under normal circumstances would have
taken twelve hours lasted four days and three nights.
Fifty people were crowded into each car. On both
sides near the ceiling were small barred windows. We
took turns standing on our knapsacks to peek out.

Once in a while the train would come to a stop,
always outside of cities, and stand on a siding for
hours. We traveled mostly at night. At some stops an
SS man would bring us a pail of water.

One morning when I gazed out of the window a
mountain range came into view. Suddenly I knew
where we were. I woke Carl. We had just passed
Teplitz.

An hour later the train stopped. It was indeed

Theresienstadt. I had passed through the small town many times on the road from our home town to Prague. There were narrow cobblestoned streets, a town square with a city hall, the obligatory Catholic church, and a few stores; the rest were garrison buildings. No one ever bothered to stop there while passing through on a journey to some other place. Theresienstadt had again become a place to be passed through—but this time as a transit camp for Jews being sent to the east.

Topping the steep hill on the outskirts of town was the Kleine Festung (the Little Fortress). The Republic of Czechoslovakia had used the Little Fortress as a military prison. Once the Germans occupied the country, they found its dungeons ideally suited for their purposes. The garrison below was used to house the Jews who had been arriving from all over Western Europe.

The car doors were unlocked and we were ordered out. It was September 7, my twenty-fifth birthday.

Walter

No one had come to welcome me when I arrived at Camp Ritchie. It was a lovely summer day. I walked leisurely along the path leading through a meadow to the camp's entrance.

By now I had become quite familiar with army camps and their drab living quarters, and I expected the same here. I was not prepared to find myself in a place that looked more like a summer resort than a military installation. MP's were cutting flowers and soldiers were pruning fruit trees. That bucolic tableau was suddenly interrupted by the approaching sound of marching feet. A column of soldiers in black SS uniforms came goose-stepping around the corner led by an officer barking orders in German. It was chilling; for a moment I thought I was somewhere in Germany. Then they disappeared into a nearby woods. They were American soldiers posing as Germans, engaged in a field exercise.

I talked to one of the MPs. He was busy planting flowers, ignoring everything going on around him. His English had a familiar inflection. The MP had been a lawyer in Vienna. He led me to my immediate superior, Staff Sergeant Antonin Prohaska.

Prohaska was a burly, middle-aged man whose

English was pure Czech. I introduced myself in Czech. It didn't exactly bring tears to his eyes. He heard Czech spoken constantly, as well as German, French, Italian, Russian, Dutch, Norwegian.

Almost all of the camp's inmates were Europeans who had been selected from the Pentagon files. My command of German helped me to become a member of the elite group of refugees who were trained at Camp Ritchie in what was known as psychological warfare. The group I joined included writers, reporters, editors, radio announcers, artists, photographers, entertainers, technicians and actors.

We had daily courses in German army organization, principles of censorship, security against espionage, basic aerial photography identification—but, above all, interrogation of prisoners of war.

Soon I could distinguish between all the German weapons as well as the various insignias of the Wehrmacht uniform. I became an expert in the interrogation of prisoners of war. Shortly before my departure for the European theater I was promoted to sergeant. There was a raucous celebration in the mess hall, which died rather quickly when word got around that our unit would be shipped out that weekend.

My duffelbag was packed. It was the evening before our departure when I was called to report to a Captain Hans Habe, who was a distinguished German novelist. He had heard that I was an actor in civilian life and asked me to join one of the four Radio Mobile Broadcasting companies, which he had recently organized in a camp not far from Ritchie.

* * *

Strict secrecy surrounded Camp Sharpe, near Gettysburg.

Surrender broadcasts to fictitious "German troops," the writing of German leaflets to be shot by light artillery across an imaginary front, and spy activity behind enemy lines were part of our training.

Trucks with loudspeakers and transmitters were parked behind our barracks. We were testing the equipment, broadcasting within the confines of the camp. Once, one of the company's chief technicians accidentally transmitted on a frequency outside his range. The citizens of Gettysburg were mystified to hear orders over their radios "to surrender to the Americans" delivered in German.

On one field exercise we roamed for forty-eight hours through the fields and forests of Pennsylvania and Maryland to play "invasion." The German front was so carefully duplicated that some of the soldiers dressed in German uniforms not only were captured by our own units and interrogated, but also by some Gettysburg farmers, who took them for escaped POWs.

After I had graduated I applied for a three-day pass. Together with my friend Sergeant Robert Breuer I went to New York. Robert was a Viennese refugee who had escaped from Europe in the late thirties. He had good looks, a suave manner and a winning smile—all of which got him a job as a doorman at Loew's Forty-second Street Theater. In his free time he studied law. The day he was admitted to the bar he was inducted into the Army. Robert still kept a small apartment in the West Seventies.

No sooner had we showered than he called his girl-

friend, Anita. She was a model. Robert asked her to
meet him at Schrafft's on Fifth Avenue, and—by the
way—could she bring her roommate Trudie along?
It would be an ideal day for Coney Island. Trudie
had made some other arrangements for the day, but
Robert convinced her that a date with me took prece-
dence over any other commitment—and particularly
on a day when the thermometer had climbed close to
100 degrees.

Anita was a native of Germany, and she had the
most charming legs I had ever seen on a girl. But she
wasn't my girl; my girl, for the day, hadn't shown
up yet. Trudie arrived at Schrafft's half an hour late.
She was Austrian. Her eyes remainded me of Hanna's.
Trudie had received her Ph.D. in Salzburg. Now she
made a living working for publishing houses, translat-
ing German manuscripts. I listened and smiled. At
this point I didn't care what she did or for whom.

We took the subway to the beach, but Coney Island
turned out to be no relief. It seemed as if all New
York had poured onto that stretch of sand to escape
the heat and humidity of the city. Still, we managed
to find a spot where we could spread our towels.

I took the orders for soft drinks and hot dogs,
threaded my way over prostrate bodies to reach the
lunch wagon, and stood in line. I closed my eyes,
barely listening to the music that blared from a small
radio on the counter. An excited voice came on with
a news bulletin. Allied forces had landed on the
beaches of Normandy. All military personnel cur-
rently on furlough were ordered to report immediately to their units.

The announcement was repeated while I tried to weave my way among the oil-tanned bodies to our own little beachhead. By the time I reached Robert and the girls, everyone seemed to know. We took the girls back to Manhattan and said goodbye. Trudie kissed me. Anita cried. Robert and I caught the next Greyhound to Gettysburg, and five hours later we were back at Camp Sharpe.

The following morning Captain Habe informed us we might be leaving for Europe at a moment's notice. Robert and I would be two of the five thousand American soldiers on the S.S. *Aquitania*.

England was our first stop. We were quartered in Brondesbury Park, a heavily bombed section of London.

On my first pass I went to see my old school friend Herbert, now a doctor at London's Fever Hospital. After we had dinner I felt like taking a leisurely stroll through the West End. By the time I had reached the Strand, a sullen, thick fog had descended. Strict blackout was enforced. Once in a while I heard an explosion and the rumblings of an ambulance or a fire truck pushing its way through the fog. From somewhere came the soft strains of music. I recognized the melody. When I saw a soldier passing by I grabbed him.

"Where are we here?"

"That's the Savoy Hotel, mate," the British soldier said.

The Savoy. That must be Jack Hilton's band.

I hummed the familiar song, "Good Night, Sweetheart," and in a flash I saw myself and Hanna back in my room in Teplitz long, long ago, welcoming the New Year—the year that was destined to separate us forever.

Hanna

We could barely crawl out of the car. We had gone for four days and three nights without food and only an occasional cup of water. The stench had been nauseating. I became dizzy taking my first breath of fresh air. Here I was back again in Czechoslovakia, in Theresienstadt, only one hour from Teplitz. It was from Theresienstadt that my parents had written their last post card. Could they still be here?

SS men and Jewish police herded us into a large hall. Men and women were separated. We had to completely undress while policewomen searched our clothes for hidden money and jewelry. Then they went through our knapsacks. Whatever they considered of value was thrown into a large cardboard box, which was quickly filled with fountain pens, watches, medicine, money and jewelry. Then came the delousing. Theresienstadt, with its century-old buildings, was alive with vermin. The air reeked of garbage, excrement and disinfectant.

Carl was waiting for me in front of the delousing barracks. Each garrison building (*Kaserne*) had a name. They all looked alike and were spread out over a few blocks. I was assigned to the Hamburger Kaserne, Karl to the Hannover.

The Hamburger, like all the others, was a grimy three-story structure built around a courtyard. Men and women were housed in separate quarters. The ground floors used to be stables. Now they, as well as all other floors, were crowded with three-decker bunks. But there were already so many people in the building that the women of our transport had to sleep on the floor in the attic. The stinking straw mattresses we were given were infested with bedbugs. Carl got a bunk in the stable of the Hannover.

One part of the old town of Theresienstadt had been declared a ghetto by the Germans. There, during the daytime, we were allowed to move around freely. Narrow cobblestoned streets were lined with old houses. In the center of town was the square with some stores, the doors and windows boarded up, a Catholic church, a savings bank, the *Sokolovna* (meeting hall) and a coffee house. Every available building had been converted into barracks. Some of them, exclusively for the very old, were crammed with bunks; here, helpless old people died daily in their dank, squalid quarters. Their food rations were even smaller than ours. They were starving to death.

Although no barbed-wire fences surrounded us, the borderlines of the ghetto were strictly defined. Any attempt to leave that area was punishable by death. Part of the border was an old brick wall. Some sections were marked with a wooden fence. From the outside the entire area was guarded by SS men and Czech police. Inside, the Jewish camp police patrolled the ghetto and were held responsible with their lives for any escape attempt. On top of a hill was the Kleine

Festung. Inmates who committed "crimes" against the Germans were taken there. It was a place from which no one ever returned.

The camp was run by the *Ältestenrat*, a council consisting of the elders among Jewish community leaders from Prague, Berlin and Vienna. They had powers— limited powers. However, they were under strict SS orders to enforce all the countless and ever-changing German edicts.

We knew already the fiendish ways the Germans operated. Jew was set against Jew, though all of us were destined for the same fate. Those inmates chosen by the Germans to be in charge usually had better living conditions for themselves and their families. More important, they were able to avoid or at least to postpone being sent on transports out of Theresienstadt. Their temporary power made them arrogant and at times corrupt. To make matters worse, a ridiculous chauvinism existed. Here the majority were Czechs who treated every foreigner with contempt. The terror of deportation to the east, however, hung over everyone in Theresienstadt. No one was safe, not even the *Ältestenrat*.

In 1941 the Germans had proclaimed Theresienstadt a ghetto for all Jews from Czechoslovakia, as well as for Jewish World War I officers who had fought for the fatherland. Furthermore, it was supposed to become a relocation center for prominent Jews from Germany and German-occupied countries. Well-known scientists, university professors, artists and musicians had been deported to Theresienstadt.

They were called *Prominente* and for a while were safe from transports to the east. Some even had better living quarters: a small room where they lived with their families. The Germans had gone to great pains to make Theresienstadt seem like an ideal Jewish settlement.

I was told that in June, two months before our arrival, the Germans had started a radical *Verschöne-rung* (beautification) of Theresienstadt. The streets were cleaned up, the fronts of buildings were painted, and a children's playground was erected, complete with swings, a merry-go-round and sandboxes. The coffeehouse was furnished with tables and chairs. The shelves of the empty general store were filled with all kinds of merchandise.

The cause of this activity was the expected visit of representatives from the International Red Cross.

A transport of thousands of sick and aged inmates left Theresienstadt for Auschwitz just days before the delegation arrived.

Theresienstadt had become a Potemkin Village with everyone playing his part. The Jews were forewarned only to answer positively any questions posed to them. The SS commandant guided the visitors, showing them only what he wanted them to see, and they in turn believed what they saw. This cynical lie was meant to calm any suspicion among the non-Jewish Czech population, as well as the Allies; Czech Red Cross teams visited here from time to time. But, in fact, inmates had been dying here by the thousands; some of neglect and starvation, others of disease. The same wooden carts that carried the dead to the crematorium were used for bread delivery—frequently at the same time.

After our arrival in the barracks Carl and I went to the administration building, the *Sekretariat*, to find out about my family. With typical German thoroughness, files were kept on all inmates. This office was run by some of the privileged prisoners. I learned that my parents and my brother had been deported in December 1943. Both my grandmothers had died in Theresienstadt. I had been prepared for the worst, but it shocked me terribly. My father's mother must have been almost ninety years old, and Grandmother Birnbaum had been eighty-four.

I looked for other relatives and was overjoyed to find that Uncle Sigmund, my father's older brother, and his wife, Aunt Rosie, were still in Theresienstadt. He was in the TB barracks, where visits were only allowed from four to six o'clock.

Carl and I went to find my aunt. It was the middle of the day; the room was dark. My aunt was sitting on a bunk. I recognized her instantly. She sat there, staring into space. Aunt Rosie was about fifty years old. She had been a beautiful woman. Now her hair was white, and deep lines showed in her face. I knew she had been suffering from glaucoma for many years. I touched her hand and softly called her name.

"Aunt Rosie—it's Hanna."

"Hannerl, you are here?"

"Yes, Aunt Rosie."

"I can't believe it." A few tears trickled down her cheeks. "Your uncle will be happy. As long as your parents were here we saw them every day. They worried about you, they were afraid you would come through here."

She explained that they had been in the same transport from Prague. The reason they were still in Theresienstadt was Uncle Sigmund's Iron Cross, First Class from World War I. Officers with these decorations had so far been exempt from deportations to the east.

"I heard you are married now, Hannerl," Aunt Rosie said. "Where is your husband?"

"Right here, Auntie Rosie."

Carl learned over and kissed her on the cheek.

She smiled. "Sit down here, Carl." She motioned him to sit next to her. "I am completely blind," she said. Her hands groped for him, and her fingers caressed his face. "You're a fine young man. And I hope you know what a wonderful girl you married. How old are you?"

"Twenty-six," Carl said.

"Twenty-six," she repeated. "That's exactly how old our Kurt was."

Kurt was her only son, one of my favorite cousins. Long ago my parents had written to me that he had been killed. I hoped to spare her the anguish of telling the story again, but she had turned to Carl and seemed quite determined.

"When the Germans occupied Teplitz, he fled. He told us that he would try to cross the border into Switzerland. We gave him all the money we had, but it was of no use. They caught him. Six weeks later we found out. We got a card. Neatly printed—you

know how neat they are. He had died in Mauthausen. They wrote us just one line: 'Died in Mauthausen.' "
We sat silent.
"Can we go to Uncle Sigmund now?" I got up.
"Of course, Hannerl. He has TB, you know. He'll be so happy to see you, if one can be happy to see a loved one in a place like this."

The following morning Carl was sent to work in the lumber yard. My friend Eva from Westerbork and I, along with most of the women of our transport, were assigned to the *Putzkolonne* (cleanup crew). We were sent to the hospital, located in the Hohenelbe Kaserne, another garrison. We scrubbed floors all day long. The large wards were filled with countless sick and ailing patients, lying in two-decker bunks. A few partitioned spaces served as doctors' offices. Nurses wore improvised uniforms, doctors had white coats. There was a limited amount of medication available.
At noon we rushed back to the Hamburger Kaserne for our meal. Compared to Westerbork, the food ladeled into our bowls was far superior; but the portions were minuscule. It only titillated our craving. The first day we had a kind of stew, the next day some soup, once we had cabbage, and at one time a small *buchtel*, a Czech dessert made of yeast dough. We dreamed of food and went into elaborate fantasies about how to procure it. Food was all we could talk about. Inmates who worked in the camp council, barracks leaders, the kitchen personnel, the camp police and a few privileged others at times got extra portions. They were envied by the rest of the inmates.

Their friendships were desired, favors were asked but were often denied. They were hated, sometimes unjustifiably, sometimes with reason. To a certain extent they had power over life and death, decided whether an inmate was absolutely essential to Theresienstadt, or was expendable and could be sent to the east. Theresienstadt was terrible, but everyone tried desperately to stay: anything was better than Auschwitz.

At night hunger and the ceaseless biting of bedbugs would keep us awake. Worse was the complete hopelessness of our lives. The near-stupor of camp existence had set in long ago in Westerbork. Apathy mixed with fear of the next day, or maybe the next week, was with us constantly. Lying awake I could hear moaning. Once in a while someone sobbed. Where could they still find tears?

I met many old friends from Teplitz. Now we found out more about Auschwitz. The stories were terrifying. Thousands who had been deported to Auschwitz, so it was rumored, had been killed on arrival.

One day I ran into Leah, one of my closest childhood friends. We were terribly happy to see each other again. We sat down on the threshold of the entrance to an old house. I told her I was happily married. We talked about Walter, whom she had known well. She told me all about her family and mentioned that her husband was employed in the kitchen as a baker.

"A baker—how wonderful," I cried, and spontaneously threw my arms around her.

She moved away suddenly.

"How lucky you are," I cried, trying to ignore the change in her.

"Yes," she said matter-of-factly, "I am lucky . . ." She got up. "I must go now," she said. "Hope to see you soon again." And she walked away.

The constant yearning for food, the hard work, the ever-present fear of being sent on a transport, the overwhelming squalor of Theresienstadt made me despair. I felt weak, sick, and fainted every day. I had made an appointment with a Jewish doctor at the hospital and asked him to interrupt my pregnancy.

"Quite impossible," he said. "I'd jeopardize my own life if I did that. It's against regulations. Too bad you didn't think of the consequences earlier."

It was one of those days that left me feeling completely without hope. I could not face Carl. I could not face the barracks. I walked around aimlessly. It was only the inevitable hunger that finally propelled me to join the queue for the evening meal—a cup of ersatz coffee and a slice of bread.

A slim girl stood in line before me. She lifted her hand and arranged her hair, and it was that gesture that made me cry out, "Lilo!" She whirled around. I had never counted on seeing Lilo again, but here she was, her lovely face radiant as always. We got our coffee, sat down, and talked.

Lilo and Michael had been in Theresienstadt for three months. They were Prominente. Michael sang at concerts in the camp. Nothing could dampen Lilo's high spirits. Her will to survive, her buoyant opti-

mism in the face of catastrophe were disarming and
uplifting. She had it from authoritative sources (in
camp lingo these rumors were called *Bonkes*) that
the Germans were in retreat on all fronts and that
most of the country had been wiped out by air
attacks.

We did not work on Sundays. Carl and I took our
blankets and went up to the *Bastei*, the bastion part of
the ancient city wall, overgrown with grass, moss
and a few bushes. Many others were there already.
From the top of the slope we could look into the free
world. At the horizon we saw the Mittelgebirge, a
mountain range where I hiked with my parents when
I was a child. I started to cry as I explained to Carl
the names of each mountain. There was the Borschen,
a craggy stone mountain that looked like a lion, and
the Milleschauer, where every first of May my father
would hike with us through the endless fields of
blooming fruit trees until we got to the summit. I
pointed out the steeple of a church behind the fields.
It was Leitmeritz, the town where Walter had his
first engagement as an actor.

    To be so close to everything that only a few years
ago meant an ordinary life—joys, maybe even at
times a routine existence—was unbearable and filled
me with rage. In the distance I saw a farmer and a
child walking along a field. I cursed them.

The Germans always picked Jewish High Holidays
for raids, deportations and executions. On the eve of
Rosh Hashanah, September 18, 1944, Carl was noti-

fied to be ready the next morning for a transport to
an eastern labor camp. Eva's father and many of our
Dutch friends had also received their deportation
orders. It was an all-male transport. Women and
children, so we heard, were soon to follow. We wanted
to believe it. We all lived on hope, and some on
prayers.

The day we had been so desperately trying to avoid
for the last two years had finally come. There was
nothing we could do. What made us believe our fate
would be different? Carl's entire barracks was going
on transport the next day. I smuggled myself inside
and spent the last night with him. It was strictly
forbidden for women to stay at night in the men's
quarters or vice versa. When the doors were locked,
I saw other wives who had also remained with their
men. It seemed no one cared any longer. What more
could they do to us? The silence of the barracks was
only broken by an occasional whisper. Carl worried
more about me and my pregnancy than about himself. I tried to convince him I might be able to stay
on in Theresienstadt until the baby was born.

In the dank light of morning we held on to each
other for the last time. With dry eyes I watched his
lanky figure disappear, becoming one with the cluster
of other deportees moving toward the waiting train.

Ten days later, on the eve of Yom Kippur, I was
handed the dreaded "gray card," the size of an ordinary post card. I had to report at six in the morning
the following day to be deported to the east. The
card said I would be reunited with my husband. It
was a transport made up entirely of women and

children. Many of my friends from Westerbork were going with me.

I said goodbye to Uncle Sigmund and Aunt Rosie. Then I went to see Lilo. Michael, in spite of being "prominent," had left with Carl. Lilo was busy packing her few belongings. She broke the silence with a forced little laugh: "Here we go again! Not to worry, we'll be with our men, that's all that matters."

Early the next morning we assembled in the courtyard of the Hamburger. Each name was checked off a list. I held hands with Lilo. Eva, close to me, in turn held her mother's and sister's hands. It had become terribly important not to lose one another. Someone put a piece of cardboard with a crudely painted number around my neck. I was completely numb. The crowd pushed and shoved me in the direction of the train station.

A man embraced me. There were tears in his eyes. He belonged somewhere in my past, but at the moment I didn't recognize him. Then suddenly it came to me—it was Mr. Neubauer, my employer in Karlsbad. I had seen him once in Theresienstadt. What was he doing at the station? Was he one of the men who had train duty?

I was pushed into a regular third-class car. More and more people were shoved in. Lilo pulled me down on a wooden bench; another woman landed on top of me. The windows were blacked out. People were calling names to find out whether their relatives or friends were somewhere in the car. Children cried. By the time the train started to move most of the women had calmed down. Since we were allowed to carry only one knapsack, everybody wore as much clothing as possible. We could barely move in the darkened car. At the rear was a toilet, which soon became unusable. We did not talk much. Even Lilo was quiet. Occasionally one of the children cried— for food, or water, or just out of misery.

It was the morning of the following day when the train came to its final stop. The doors were unlocked. I closed my eyes to avoid being blinded by the daylight. The first thing I saw were chimneys belching fire and smoke.

A bullhorn cut through the morning mist: "*Raus!*" (Get out!) Male prisoners in blue-and-white striped uniforms pulled us out of the car. Some people had died during the trip, and their bodies were piled on the muddy ground. SS men were everywhere. Everything was gray. The sky blended into the gray landscape. Cement towers with searchlights rose above the high barbed-wire fences. Behind the fences I saw stone barracks, long barnlike structures with narrow openings near the roof. Even the rain that was falling looked gray.

Kapos, as the men in the striped prison uniforms were called, unloaded our knapsacks. I quickly tried to grab mine. A Kapo pushed me aside roughly. I was not allowed to touch my only remaining belongings. Everything that still tied me to my past was in that sack. Photographs of my parents, my brother, my grandmother, Carl, and, of course, the Ecuadorian passport.

SS men with fierce-looking dogs on leashes shouted at us to fall into two lines and to get moving. In the distance I saw an SS officer, in black uniform, giving commands with a flick of a hand. With merely a glance he made his selection: Left—right. Left—right. I stood about two hundred feet from the officer when I noticed a Kapo moving between the lines, obviously searching for someone. He stopped for a moment when he passed me and whispered, "Hanna—remember? I'm Jan."

He was one of our friends from Amsterdam. I never would have recognized him in his striped prison garb with his shaven, skull-like head.

"Jan—where are we?" I whispered.

"Auschwitz."

"Jan, I'm pregnant . . . if they ask me—?"

He shook his head violently. "Not a word, for God's sake." His eyes ran quickly over my body. "It does not show. Just try to look as healthy and strong as possible."

He was about to move on.

"Jan, have you seen Carl?"

He shrugged his shoulders and went on. Had he not heard me? I was hoping he would return, but he never did.

In front of me stood Lilo with a friend and her two children. Greta, the mother, carried her little girl in her arms. Her three-year-old son started to cry; he also wanted to be held. Lilo picked him up.

Next to me was Eva, in back of us her mother and sister. Again we all tried to stay together. Slowly we moved closer to the table with the SS officers.

The dogs strained the leashes held by the SS men who were walking alongside the columns of prisoners.

We were not allowed to talk. Some children whimpered. The SS officer pointed to Lilo to go to the left with Greta and her little daughter. He must have assumed the child Lilo carried was her own.

Now I faced the officer. He gave me a swift, cold look and pointed to the right. Head erect I moved to the right column; so did Eva and her mother and sister. I hated to be separated from Lilo; we waved to each other. She mouthed the words "See you later," and disappeared.

We were led away to the "sauna," a large stone building. Inside we were ordered to undress and to put our clothing into neat piles. All married women had to hand over their wedding rings. Kapos and SS men watched us. Petrified, we looked at the men. They kept yelling at us to move faster and stand in rows of ten. Now, completely naked, we were inspected once more. Some older women were taken to one side. We did not realize this was the second selection and that we had survived. Still naked and shivering we were chased out of the building into another "sauna." The entire procedure was so terrifying that my mind became completely numb.

We joined another long line; women Kapos grabbed us and started to shave our heads. They pulled the hair with one hand, while cutting with the other, using large scissors. The next Kapo shaved off with a razor whatever hair was left, including the pubic area. We looked at each other—it was an unbearable sight. I did not recognize Eva. Suddenly everyone looked alike—bald, naked, ugly.

Then we were taken to the showers. The water was

ice-cold. Teeth chattering, our bodies a deep blue, we were pushed naked and wet outside; then we were rushed to another barracks. On the way we passed a detachment of German soldiers. They stared at us and laughed. Finally we were given some castoff clothing. I got an old torn summer dress, five sizes too large. We never saw our own things again.

Hundreds of women were housed in one barracks. In the center, through the length of the *Block*, as the building was called, ran a two-foot-high brick divider. Both sides of the barracks were lined with three-tiered wooden bunks. The space between the bunks was too narrow to sit. Ten people were crowded into two connecting bunks. We were about six hundred women in our barracks. A huge sign, ARBEIT MACHT FREI (work liberates) had been painted in Gothic lettering on the rear wall. I was lucky enough to stay with my friends from Westerbork—all except Lilo and Greta. I had no idea yet what had happened to them, or the other women and children who had been in our transport.

One woman barracks leader (*blockova*) was in charge of each barracks. Blockovas, usually Poles or Slovaks, most of them not Jewish, had been in Auschwitz a long time. They were the elite. They had kept their hair, wore warm clothing, leather shoes or boots, and most of them were well fed. On one arm numbers were tattooed. On a ribbon around the neck they carried a whistle.

We were treated with utter disdain, like cattle on the way to the slaughterhouse. The behavior of the blockovas had been honed by years of imprisonment at Auschwitz. Some of these women had been criminals. Even the few Jews among them had gone through such deprivations and fights for survival that they were now incapable of any feeling short of self-preservation. All of them, like the Kapos, had achieved their positions in the camp partly through elimination and seniority and partly by sexual relationships with higher-ups, both hetero- and homosexual. They were not prostitutes; they just tried to survive. At Auschwitz, food and warm clothing were the keys to survival.

Our barracks had at one time been stables for horses. Narrow windows under the roof, almost obscured by dirt, gave the interior whatever daylight there was. At the front, a small area was separated into a makeshift room; it belonged to the blockova. A garbage can was placed in the rear of the barracks at nighttime to be used as a toilet. One bucket for all of us. It was called the *Scheisskübel* (shit bucket).

At four o'clock in the morning the blockova blew her whistle to get us ready for *Zählappell* (roll call). We wore *Klompen*, Dutch wooden shoes, much too large for us. Often someone ended up with either two left or two right ones. We had no socks or stockings, so walking was difficult, running a torture. The blockovas constantly forced us to run. Speed was an obsession in Auschwitz. Roll call was held outside on the Lagerstrasse, a muddy thoroughfare running through the center of each compound. Even though we stood in rows of ten, the blockova always seemed to come up with the wrong numbers. She was responsible for the correct count of inmates. If anyone was missing, she would be punished, possibly even killed. Many times the count was incorrect because someone had died during the night. We would stand in the cold and mud for hours, rain pelting on our shaved heads. Roll call sometimes took as long as three hours. Finally the SS would arrive, at times with their dogs, check the numbers of prisoners, and we would be chased back into the barracks.

I fainted frequently. We had arranged that during roll call one of my friends would stand in back of me and hold me up if I collapsed. Once the blockova noticed one of my fainting spells. Eva was not able to catch me fast enough. The blockova held me with one hand, while with the other she kept slapping my face. She broke my nose, but, as I realized later, her on-the-spot brutality probably saved my life. When I came to, I saw Eva crying. I had not felt a thing.

After roll call we were taken to the latrines. We all had dysentery. One barracks in each compound served as a latrine. Once, sometimes twice a day, we were taken there by our blockova. We were never allowed out of our barracks alone. The woman in charge of the latrine was called an *abortova*, a Polish word. It was an "exalted" position. She lived in the front part of the latrines, had a bunk for herself and a small iron stove, where she actually cooked cabbage or potatoes. The stench was nauseating. There were two rows of dirty wooden holes. The smell of human excrement was mingled with the reek of disinfectant. The abortova, who was not Jewish, would walk up and down, equipped with the ever-present whip, hit-

ting us if we were not actually sitting down in the
filth.

There was no work assigned to us, contrary to the
ludicrous slogan about "work liberating" us. Around
noontime we were given a cup of poisonous borscht
in a wooden bowl. In the early evening the ritual of
the roll call was repeated. The official language in
our barracks was Slovakian, since our blockova was a
Slovak. When she got up on the brick divider, blew
her whistle and yelled *Ticho*, every Dutch, Czech,
Polish, French, Hungarian or German woman in my
barracks knew it meant "Silence!" Naturally, whenever she had to answer an SS man, she spoke German.

It was at Auschwitz that the thought of suicide
began to preoccupy me. All I had to do was run outside and touch one of the electrified barbed-wire
fences that were all around us. Many had chosen this
way out, but were sometimes shot by the watchtower
guards before they could even reach the wire. The
option became increasingly tempting.

Very soon after our arrival I had heard about the
gas chambers, which were built like the other "sau-
nas," but their showerheads were fitted for gas instead of water. I knew the forever-smoking chimneys
were the crematoria. I was convinced that neither
my parents nor my brother could possibly have survived Auschwitz. Maybe, just maybe, Carl had a
chance; when he was deported from Theresienstadt
he was still a strong-looking young man. Had he
escaped a selection? But even if he had, for how long?
At roll call I sometimes could see through the barbed

wire into the next compound. The prisoners standing there looked even worse than we did.

Auschwitz was divided into many smaller compounds (*Lager*), each encircled with barbed wire as a separate unit. Some were given letters of the alphabet (mine was *B Lager*, or B Camp), or designated into types such as Gypsy Camp, Criminal Camp, Family Camp. The Family Camp had been established for *one* trainload of prisoners from Theresienstadt in the winter of 1943. A few Prominente with their families were included in that transport. Without having to go through the selection process, they had been taken directly to the Family Camp, where they stayed for a couple of months; then, with very few exceptions, they all had been gassed. It was just one more of the illogical incongruities of Auschwitz.

The weak or sick were sent to the gas chambers sooner or later. Children were killed immediately. To have a child was as good as a death sentence. When I thought of Lilo carrying Greta's child in her arms, I could only hope that at the right time she explained the circumstances and was sent to another compound.

Even though we knew the truth by now, some of us refused to accept it. Intelligent and rational people would take refuge in fantasies, thinking that maybe the women and children were still alive.

On October 15, 1944, two weeks after our arrival in Auschwitz, the blockova called out my name.

I was petrified. Only the few friends who shared nearby bunks knew who I was. Who else would know? What would they want of me? I noticed a male prisoner standing with our blockova and talking to her. He was no ordinary prisoner.

In Auschwitz a weird caste system prevailed. Some of the inmates were first-class citizens. They wore custom-tailored striped prison jackets, and shoes that actually fit; and even the red line on the back of their uniform was drawn symmetrically, with a ruler. These privileged inmates were either blockovas, Kapos, or doctors and nurses.

"Here," I called out, and already regretted it. How could one trust anybody in this place? I climbed from my bunk and walked up to the blockova and her visitor. He was a man in his forties, though in Auschwitz one never could tell a person's age. There were girls in their twenties who looked like wilted old women.

"Are you Hanna Benjamin?" the man said.

I nodded.

"Have you a brother?"

"Yes . . . I have a brother."

"What's his name?"

"Friedl."

The man relaxed. "I am bringing you regards from him."

I stood there, almost nude, with no hair on my skull, and started to cry.

"Your brother is in F Camp. He's a colleague of mine."

"And my parents," I sobbed. "Are they here too?"

The man shrugged. The by now familiar shrug.

"Can I see Friedl?"

"He cannot get a pass," the man said. "It's impossible for him to see you. He's a doctor in the men's sick barracks."

"How did he know I was here?"

"He heard about the transport from Theresienstadt and found out there were Dutch women on the train. Ever since, he has been trying to find out whether you were one of them. Would you like me to tell him anything for you?"

"Would it be possible to get me a piece of paper and a pencil? I would like to write a few lines to Friedl."

He went over to the blockova, who had been watching us; she found a shred of paper and the stump of a pencil. I scribbled a few lines to Friedl, telling him that I loved him and that I was strong. I mentioned my pregnancy and asked him what I should do about it. I also wished him "Happy Birthday." October 15, 1944, was his thirtieth birthday.

When the man had gone, I learned from our blockova that he was her husband. She was bitter. If caught with a message, he would have been shot on the spot. But the note was not intercepted. Friedl was able to have me transferred to the sick barracks in C Camp. My blockova took me there. I never saw Friedl.

Ever since Westerbork, I wondered why the Germans bothered to have hospitals and sick barracks, even here in Auschwitz. Why treat people, and then send them to be gassed? Every SS detachment had its own ideas how to run its concentration camp. The basic plan of each commandant was to keep his camp in existence, which meant, I suppose, that he had to keep some people alive.

A woman prison doctor, a Hungarian, performed the abortion. I was put on a kitchen table. They had no anesthetic and no sterilized instruments. I spent that night in the sick barracks. Rumors circulated there would be a "selection" the following morning.

Selections occurred at unpredictable intervals. The first one would take place upon the arrival of each incoming transport. Whenever barracks were overcrowded there would be a selection, especially in the sick barracks. Any Jewish religious holiday was unfailingly chosen for a selection. Then there were the *Sonderaktionen* (special projects), retaliations for incidents happening in the outside world. It could be that in one of the occupied countries a German had been murdered, or a building blown up by the local underground. Or even worse, a prisoner may have attempted to escape from Auschwitz.

The sick barracks were built like all the others, but were not overcrowded. Two patients shared one bunk and one blanket. This was an improvement from the nine people with whom I had to share my bunk in B Camp.

That evening I was certain I was going to die. I thought of all the people I had loved and would never see again. I even fleetingly thought of Walter. It had been my eighteenth day in Auschwitz. Never before had I felt so abandoned. I had not heard from Friedl again and I began to worry whether he was still alive. In Auschwitz, two days were an eternity.

Would Carl be able to survive here? Had Jan's cynical shrug meant that he was dead? Had the reaction of Friedl's colleague, when I inquired about my parents, meant the same thing? Were they all dead? After a while I felt strangely at peace. Death by gas could not take too long. A deep breath—and it would be over. No more fear, no more degradation, no more hunger, no more cold.

My bed partner was softly wailing in a mixture of Polish and Yiddish. I put my arms around her and tried to comfort her. I don't know whether she understood my words, but she stopped her lament, and like a frightened child, clung to me. For a time all was quiet. Then we heard a baby crying.

A nurse stood in front of our bunk holding a newborn child, wrapped in pink crepe paper. My bed-partner's face lit up. She stretched out her hands for the baby and pressed it to her bosom. It was her first —and probably her last—look at her daughter. Did they have blue paper for baby boys?

Dawn came, and with it, the SS. Everyone in the barracks was ordered to get out of bed. Two SS men, accompanied by Dr. Perl, the doctor who had performed my abortion, were walking slowly from bunk to bunk. This time I knew what the selection was about. Those too weak or too sick to stand at attention were chased by Kapos to one corner of the barracks. Anyone who lingered was beaten with leather whips. The women screamed. A few of us were permitted to stay; the majority were taken away, among them the Polish woman who had been my bed partner.

Soon after, the entire sick barracks was emptied and I was returned to B Camp. I immediately looked for my friends. Only Eva was there. She had given up hope of ever seeing me again. While I was away, her mother and sister had left on a transport with a group of other women, supposedly going to a German labor camp. Eva and I promised each other never to be separated again. To survive in this world of utter anonymity it had become a necessity to have a friend near you.

Those endless roll calls became even more disastrous for me. I was desperately sick. I ran a fever, and at times was delirious. Eva would not leave my side. It always rained; the rain had become a part of our bodies.

Three weeks after our arrival in Auschwitz Eva and I, along with a number of other prisoners from our compound, were moved again. B Camp was being liquidated. We held hands in desperate fear of being separated. As we were being herded out of our barracks we were convinced that this was the end. However, we were taken to a different compound, the FKL (*Frauen Konzentrations Lager*), the Women's Concentration Camp. Again we had to share our bunk with nine other women. Most of the inmates in the FKL were criminals. Long ago the Germans had emptied women's penitentiaries everywhere and sent the inmates to Auschwitz. Our blockova was a murderess. Some of the women had been there many months, some even years. The predominant language was Polish. The blockova, assisted by a couple of *stubovas* (helpers), kicked and dragged us bodily when we were too weak to stand up for roll call. They hit us with leather whips that had pieces of iron tied to the thongs.

The front part of our barracks was partitioned off by a beaded curtain. This room was furnished. It had beds, real beds covered with pink bedspreads. There was a rug on the floor, and pillows were scattered everywhere. A fringed lampshade hung over a table lamp. In one corner stood a potbellied stove. A group of inmates were sitting around it. They wore dainty panties and bras—nothing else. They all had hair. We were, of course, not allowed near that part of the barracks, and only passed it on our way to and from roll calls.

Our stay in the FKL lasted about a week. Each morning we wondered whether we would see the sky another day, and each day brought new rumors. During the nights, we had been hearing the sounds of planes flying over the camp. Occasionally the ground shook from nearby artillery fire. It seemed that the Russian front was coming closer. There was also talk that Auschwitz would be evacuated. Again we were never allowed out of the barracks except for roll call and the trip to the latrines. I thought and worried a great deal about Friedl. I had no more messages, no further sign he was still alive. If he was, he might not even know where to find me.

One morning our blockova ordered us all out of our bunks. Outside we heard whistles blowing, voices giving orders. There was fear and anxiety in the air. All Jewish prisoners were rushed outside to the "sauna." The doors were closed and the showers were turned on; they released water. Afterward, still naked, we were taken to a nearby warehouse, a large barracks stuffed with clothing. Each of us received underwear, a dress, a coat and a pair of shoes. A couple of blockovas brushed a crude large red line of paint on the back of our coats. Each of us was given a hunk of bread. I looked at the women around me. Most were about my age. A Kapo blew his whistle, and all of us —about five hundred—were marched to the station. A row of cattle cars was waiting and we were rushed inside.

The doors were slammed and locked from outside. For hours the train just stood there. Where were we going? Would we really leave this hell alive? And why had we been spared? It was quite possible that the authorities would change their minds and march us into camp again or take us somewhere and shoot us. Then at night the train began to move. When we had received our clothes in the warehouse we had been told we were going to a labor camp in Austria. At the time, we did not believe it, since we had heard so many similar rumors before. The train moved slowly, almost reluctantly. Finally it gathered speed; we really were leaving Auschwitz. Even though we were starving and freezing, we felt almost cheerful.

We stopped frequently during the day and moved mostly at night. On the third day a Czech girl yelled, "Look, we are in Mährisch-Ostrau. I can see my house from here!" Between the wooden boards on the sides of the car were slits, large enough to see flashes of the outside. Everyone scrambled to get a look. I saw Czech inscriptions: MORAVSKA OSTRAVÁ.

At our next stop we could read the sign above the station: WIENER NEUSTADT. Outside it was raining; the water seeped into the car. We spent another night locked in the train. The cold and hunger were awful; no one even had the strength to talk. The following morning the train stopped and the doors were opened.

We were in Vöcklabruck, a small town in Upper Austria.

Walter

September mildness hovered over the Normandy coast when we drove off the LCT onto Omaha Beach. We passed burned-out Sherman tanks and disabled jeeps. On the bluff above we could see a number of huge cement towers, pockmarked by shells, their silent cannon pointed toward the sea. A few MPs were directing traffic. None of us talked. We drove up the bluff, looking for a place to bivouac. A field kitchen was set up.

Early next morning our motorized column left in the direction of Paris. All day long we drove through the battered and devastated French countryside. It was late when we reached the outskirts of Paris. I had never been in Paris and would have loved to spend a few days there. But we only stopped overnight and left early next day, driving through Châlons-sur-Marne, Verdun and Metz to reach our ultimate destination—the Duchy of Luxembourg.

To me Luxembourg was little more than the backdrop of an operetta by Franz Lehár, *The Count of Luxembourg*, a charming, schmaltzy musical that had been part of the repertory of every provincial European theater. But what we found when we entered the capital, also called Luxembourg, bore little resemblance to the fluff of the operetta.

The town did not show the ravages of four years of Nazi occupation. But the scars were there. Here I got firsthand reports from people whose relatives had been conscripted for foreign labor and sent to Germany. The small Jewish community had been deported to Poland, except for a handful who had gone into hiding and survived.

We were warmly welcomed, and though the stores were empty and restaurants offered little choice of food, many of us were invited into the homes of the Luxembourgers. Part of my company was billeted in an old patrician villa that previously had been requisitioned by the Germans.

Radio Luxembourg was one of the most powerful transmitters in Europe. The Germans had retreated shortly before and had pulled out in such a hurry that they left the radio station and its transmitter in excellent working condition. We took over the station at once. Our news team wrote and translated the daily news and bulletins into German, French, Italian, Russian, Czech and Dutch. Different announcers were broadcasting around the clock. I transmitted the news in German three times daily. There were musical interludes during the news breaks. Local news was broadcast in Luxembourgoise, a melange of French and German. Twice weekly the local string orchestra gave a live performance.

One of the most successful operations was a program called "Letters to and from Home." We had come into possession of sacks of undelivered mail left behind by the fleeing Germans. These letters from soldiers' wives and relatives, as well as those written by the soldiers to their families, gave us an inestimable insight into the morale of the Germans. Some of these letters were read over our station and in turn prompted the Germans to tune in, hoping in this roundabout way to hear from their loved ones.

From time to time we drove our mobile loudspeaker trucks to the front lines to urge the enemy to surrender. We shot leaflets, called *Passierscheine*, into German territory, guaranteeing safe-conduct, good food and no reprisals. The operation proved highly successful and deserters came in great numbers.

One day in the middle of December, intelligence headquarters informed us that the enemy had dropped parachutists over the duchy, supposedly former German-Americans whose IDs were brilliantly forged and who spoke English faultlessly. Special security measures were taken to arrest any suspicious-looking soldiers.

The MPs had strict orders not to trust an ID or even dogtag of anyone. In order to establish true identity a number of questions were posed that only a genuine American could have answered. One evening a member of my company, Corporal Loewenbein, a musician of studious appearance from Berlin, accompanied a German prisoner to headquarters for interrogation. They spoke English—the German almost perfectly, Loewenbein with a heavy accent. A tough MP stopped them. He listened to Loewenbein suspiciously and asked him, "How many homers did Babe Ruth hit?" Loewenbein was stumped. "What's the name of Li'l Abner's girlfriend?" Loewenbein stared uncomfortably at the sergeant. For a moment it was touch-and-go for Loewenbein. Only when the sergeant was about to nail him with the third question,

"Who's Dr Pepper?," did Loewenbein smile and answer in his most fastidious manner, "Sergeant, it is not *who* is Dr Pepper—but *what* is Dr Pepper!" The sergeant laughed and let them pass.

Ten days before Christmas, the Germans launched their last desperate counteroffensive. My friend Robert Breuer returned that day from a reconnaissance trip with the sinister report that "the sons of bitches have recovered forty kilometers of ground."

We celebrated part of Christmas in the basement of Radio Luxembourg, but broadcasting never stopped. We wore steel helmets and kept our guns near our microphones. At one point we learned that the Germans were within three miles of the station. That was the closest I had ever come to actual combat. Soon after, the enemy was forced into permanent retreat.

One morning in January, Breuer came rushing into Studio 1 holding an issue of the *Luxemburger Wort* in his hand. All color had drained from his face. The whole front page carried a photo with the headline NAZIS GAS JEWS IN DEATH VANS. The photo showed a long line of naked men, women and children. SS troops, their guns drawn, were pushing the victims into a huge van.

A taste of bile rose in my throat. Maybe, I thought, this was a single incident, maybe one of our own propaganda fabrications. I forced myself to look once more at that photo, studying the faces of the SS and their victims. No, this picture couldn't have been posed. It had actually happened. They had gassed those people. I pushed the paper away. But what I had seen couldn't be pushed away. It stayed with me all day long. It followed me into a sleepless night. I thought of all those I knew who had been unable to get out of occupied Europe. I walked the floor and opened the door to Breuer's room. He was awake. He had left all of his family in Vienna.

I thought of Hanna, and my mind began to fill with remorse and self-reproach. I talked with Breuer into the early hours of the morning. He tried to be reassuring. And he pointed out that since Hanna was married, at least she wouldn't be alone in her struggle for survival. Maybe she had gone underground in Holland. Intelligence reports confirmed that the Dutch were hiding Jews, even providing them with false identification papers. Every day more and more intelligence reports about Hitler's Final Solution filtered through. The enormity of what had gone on in the so-called labor camps was beyond imagination. Human beings, thousands, millions of them, including people I had known, had been gassed and cremated, and the killing was still going on.

Eisenhower's armies began to close in on the Rhine. At the beginning of March we had progressed to the bridge at Remagen. The bridge was captured intact and our armies moved swiftly into Germany. The day Roosevelt died, the Russians were in the suburbs of Vienna. On April 25 Russian soldiers shook hands with our soldiers on a bridge crossing the Elbe River at Torgau. Hitler, trapped in a bunker in Berlin, with the Russians only a few miles away from the Reich

Chancellery, committed suicide when he realized all was lost. On May 7 the Germans surrendered unconditionally at Reims.

The population of Luxembourg was jubilant. The war was over.

Captain Edward Rothe, a friend from Teplitz and a member of the Czech brigade, a unit of Czech exiles under British military command, was on detached duty in Luxembourg. A few days after the end of the war he was sent on special orders to Theresienstadt to talk to the survivors and get firsthand reports about the concentration camp. I asked him to look for any leads to the Kohner and Bloch families, and, of course, to find out whether anyone might have seen Hanna in Theresienstadt. I also told him that maybe Hanna had married and might have been registered under her new name. If he couldn't locate her, perhaps survivors might provide him with a clue. Every day one heard of such miracles.

Rothe returned. He had information about the two families. The Nazis had kept meticulous records. There were thousands and thousands of names listed, all those who had passed through Theresienstadt as well as those who had died there, or those who had survived. Yes, there *were* survivors. One was an elderly man, Dr. Rudolph Lederer, an eye specialist from our home town. He had remained in the camp all those years, and was still tending the sick and dying. Typhoid had infested Theresienstadt and had claimed many who were too weak to fight the disease. It was Dr. Lederer who remembered both the Blochs and Hanna; he also recalled her married name. In the records, Rothe discovered the names of Max and Hertha and Gottfried (Friedl) Bloch. And Hanna—now Hanna Benjamin—had also gone through the camp. According to the lists she went on transport on September 27, 1944—to Auschwitz. I thanked Captain Rothe. He could tell what I was thinking.

"It doesn't mean that she is dead," he said.

Hanna

Winter 1944 started early. When we arrived in Vöcklabruck on November 2, it was snowing. Water had been seeping through the roof of the cattle car, and our clothes were drenched. We shivered in the cold wind as we climbed out. The station platform was crowded with SS men and women. Dogs were barking. Guards yelled at us to fall into double lines, and began to check the numbers of prisoners from a list. As far as we could see, nobody had died during the trip.

For nearly two hours we walked through wintry fields and woods. We passed a number of red barracks surrounded by a brick wall. For a moment we thought it might be our camp. It did not look too bad. As we came closer we saw men in POW uniforms inside the compound. They were Russian prisoners. Some of them waved at us. We marched past the small village of Lenzing, with its chalet-type houses. On the horizon we saw snowcapped mountains. The sun peeked out from behind the clouds and the fresh air slowly revived us. It was certainly a change for the better. The villagers of Lenzing showed utter contempt for us. Some ignored our presence. Prisoners must have been a familiar sight to them.

Outside the village, surrounded by barbed wire, stood a partially bombed-out factory. But this time there were no watchtowers, no barracks. A dilapidated chimney belonged to the factory—not to a crematorium. This was to be our new camp. The roof had been severely damaged. Some of the windows were broken. Inside it was bitter cold. Double-decker bunks were lined up in a huge room. In the center stood a small unlit iron stove.

Each of us had a bunk to herself, a straw mattress and a horse blanket. The washroom, with a row of cold-water faucets and latrines, was in the back of the building. A smaller room served as a makeshift sick barracks. One of my fellow inmates was a young woman doctor from Prague. We were given blue-and-white striped caps and jackets. A number was sewn on each uniform; mine was 469.

At our first roll call the camp commandant, a robust, thickset *Walküre*, bellowed: "You are in Camp Lenzing, one of the camps belonging to Mauthausen. You will work in a textile mill, serving the war effort." She went on to explain that the mill was located four kilometers from the camp. We would be divided into three eight-hour shifts. Except for a cadre of camp personnel, everyone had to work in the mill.

I stood in the second row while she was talking. My knees suddenly started to buckle. Eva, standing behind me, held me up. It had not been quite two weeks since my abortion.

During the three-day train ride from Auschwitz, I had been intermittently delirious. I vaguely remembered a woman leaning against the wall of the cattle car, cradling me in her arms and speaking softly in Hungarian. I did not understand her words—but I understood the meaning.

After my fainting spell at roll call, I decided to take the risk of reporting to the sickroom. There was nothing Erna Springer, our doctor, could do for me. She had no medication, not even aspirin. I slept most of the time. When I saw an SS doctor standing at my bedside, I sat up with a start. He asked a few questions; his visit was short. After a week I felt better and joined the rest of the inmates.

The daily routine began: Up at six. Roll call. A slice of black bread and some brown liquid. Then the morning shift would leave for the factory. We would walk through the cobblestoned village of Lenzing, and along meadows, a dense forest and a small clear stream. We crossed the railway tracks and finally reached the factory. We were guarded by heavily armed SS men and women, who treated us like a dangerous band of outlaws and not walking skeletons.

The plant was a modern textile mill and spinnery; it manufactured synthetic yarn for parachutes. The personnel consisted of a few foremen from Lenzing; some foreign laborers who had been deported from their homelands to work in the factory; and then us, looking as if we had stepped out of a painting by Hieronymus Bosch. The SS watched us closely. None of us would have had the strength to break out or to sabotage the "war effort."

Ten women were detailed to each foreman, who

instructed us how to operate the intricate machinery. My friend Eva and I were assigned to the drying machine, a structure two stories high. We learned how to read and regulate the temperatures, walk along a catwalk to watch the drying yarn and check that it did not overflow the bins. I was very fortunate to be in this section of the plant. Some prisoners worked at the washing machines, where the yarn was soaked in a sulfur solution. At times they were blinded by the fumes, and their hands had open sores. To make things worse, they worked under a brutal foreman.

My foreman, Herr Ofenmüller, was a middle-aged, soft-spoken man. He soon made it clear he was no Nazi sympathizer, but an old socialist. Once in a while he slipped some of us a cooked potato. He also informed us about the latest German setbacks. He ran an incredible risk, for any verbal contact with a prisoner, outside of work orders, was strictly forbidden.

Although we were not permitted to talk among ourselves, we sometimes broke the rule. Our SS guards would be walking up and down the aisles between the machines, watching us impassively. It soon became evident that we were not really needed here. The bosses who ran the mill and the spinnery were mainly interested in keeping it going to avoid being sent to the front. Occasionally the plant had to close down for lack of fuel. To keep us busy, our guards made us dig trenches. There we stood, all skin and bones, trying to swing a pickax, which we were barely able to lift.

It rained or snowed through the damaged roof onto our bunks, and the room was bitterly cold. We never

undressed at night but slept in our clothes. Our bunks
were infested by lice; now the lice invaded our clothing and robbed us of sleep. They also caused an out-
break of typhus. We already had dysentery and
some of us were suffering from TB. The sickroom
soon became overcrowded. Those of us who were
fortunate not to catch typhus volunteered to nurse
our sick friends whenever we were not working.

Each morning at four o'clock, six prisoners pulling
a large cart would leave under armed guard to pick
up the daily food rations. Everybody was eager to be
part of the soup detail; it meant an extra portion of
soup—a treat that we shared with our sick friends.
Russian prisoners of war were in charge of the kitchen,
which was next to the mill. At times the SS women
guarding us would engage us in some kind of conversation. They would inquire about our lives before
the war. Where did we come from? What did our
fathers do for a living? When Eva once answered
that her father had owned a chain of department
stores in Germany, one SS woman sneered, "Naturally, *ein jüdischer Grossindustrieller*" (Jewish big
shot). They never talked about themselves, nor did
they mention that Germany was losing on all fronts.

Once, while waiting inside the kitchen for the
food, we spotted a garbage can filled with raw potato
peelings. We made a dive for them. When the guards
saw us eating them and stuffing some in our pockets,
they screamed at us, "*Ihr dreckigen Hunde!*" (You
dirty dogs.) They hit and kicked us furiously. "*Zu-
rück in den Eimer!*" (Back into the pail.)

Those were the same guards who an hour earlier

had spoken with us on our way to the kitchen. We had to empty our pockets and return the potato peels. What did they know about hunger?

Food. We talked about little else. We discussed how to prepare complete menus, how to fix certain dishes, including regional differences, and we salivated at the mere mention of an ingredient. We could practically taste the food.

Another diversion to help me escape the incessant misery of just staying alive was music. Eva and I played a game on our way home from work. One of us would start humming a few bars of a symphony or a concerto and the other would have to guess the composer, or carry on where the first left off. Anything that came to our minds. It took us back to a world we used to know.

One morning as we entered the factory, a group of foreign laborers stood around watching us. "Look at the poor little boy," one of them said, pointing at me. How many months had it been since I looked in a mirror? My head had been shaved in Auschwitz just five weeks earlier. I was small and skinny; did I look like a boy?

A week later one of the foreign women pushed a parcel into my hands. I was bewildered. She rushed away before I could even see her face. The contents of the package were wrapped in a letter. I opened it, and stared at a piece of bread with a slice of sausage. I quickly hid it and rushed over to Eva's place at the machine. I motioned her to follow me, and in a dark corner, after the guard had just passed, I shared the gift with my friend. We gulped down the bread and sausage. Afterward our hunger was worse. Then I tried to read the letter. Had someone sent me a message? Could it have been Carl or Friedl or some other member of my family?

The letter, written in German, made no sense at all. I showed it to Eva. During the course of the day I read the letter again and again. Finally I came to the conclusion that it contained no secret message for me. It was simply used by my benefactor, whoever she was, to wrap the sandwich in.

There was less and less food, and more and more women were dying of hunger and disease. The first death had occurred shortly after our arrival. It was a Polish woman I did not know, and we buried her in a wooden box in the courtyard of the camp. We said Kaddish (the Jewish prayer for the dead). Later on, when many more died, the SS just took their bodies away in a truck.

Still we went on, existing from day to day. One of my friends had been hiding her pregnancy. Eventually she was admitted to the sickroom. I admired her courage, and envied her. The war will be over one day soon, I thought, and she will be able to keep her child. The baby was stillborn; the mother survived.

One day an SS man on duty overheard someone calling me by my married name. He sauntered over and whispered, "Are you from Cologne?"

"I'm not, but my husband's family came from there."

"Are you related to Dr. Max Benjamin, the pediatrician?"

I nodded. "He is my father-in-law."

He seemed greatly disturbed as he walked up and down the aisle; he did not want to be noticed talking to me. Even the SS were not permitted to speak to us.

"Your father-in-law was our children's doctor. He delivered them. Once he sat up all night with my little Erich when he had scarlet fever. He did not even charge me because he knew I had lost my job. A fine man. What happened to him—and his wife?"

"What happened to them? What happened to all of us?"

"I am only doing my duty, like everyone else. Do you think I like it?" He never talked to me again.

Early one morning an accident happened. The night shift was on its way back to the camp. A heavy snowstorm turned into a sudden blizzard. The railway crossing had no barrier. No one saw or heard the approaching commuter train. Six women were killed instantly. We heard the screaming. Dogs howled. A few inmates were sent out to collect the bodies. They were all dismembered. Two of the women who had survived could not stop screaming. For days they screamed, then they were taken to nearby Mauthausen and the gas chambers.

Bread began to disappear. We would leave our bunks for a few minutes and return to find the daily bread ration gone. Who among us would do this? Certainly not Milana, everyone's friend, sweet, warm-hearted and compassionate. Someone suspected her, lifted her mattress, and there it was: a dozen pieces of dry, moldy bread, smelly and inedible. For a long time Milana was ostracized; eventually she was forgiven. But never completely.

One night in February a group of women arrived in our camp. They had been marching through the snow for two days and two nights under SS guard. Of a large transport, only twenty women had survived; the rest had died on the road. Katja, one of the survivors, was a fourteen-year-old Yugoslavian girl. Her feet were partially frozen, the toes looked like black stumps. She was lying in the sickroom, never complaining, always smiling. We found out that she had been in Auschwitz. Maybe that innocent, inane, crazy smile had saved her.

By March 1945 most of the snow had melted. Some of the Polish and Slovakian inmates knew about herbs. They had been brought up in the country and showed us city people which of the herbs sprouting in the fields were edible. Some grew right at the edge of the road, and we picked them furtively on our way to and from work. Another godsend was the sudden presence of snails. We smuggled them into the factory and cooked them in our cups over the steam of the machines. There was no longer any bread and the daily rations of soup were reduced to two spoonsful. No explanation was given.

Toward the end of April an SS man, who had never before spoken to me, told me that President Roosevelt had died. Whoever followed him, the guard declared, would make peace with Germany. The Americans and Germans would then liquidate Russia, their common enemy. Wouldn't they love that, the bastards, I thought, but what I said was: "It's quite possible."

Then she stretched our her hand to Siddy, our blockova. Siddy stood calmly, with visible disdain in her eyes, keeping her hands clasped behind her back.

That was the last we saw of the commandant and the rest of the SS guards.

We stood around numb. What would happen? Were we free? We went into the courtyard. A squadron of planes flew overhead. They had unfamiliar insignia on their wings. We waved at them. An unbelievable joy overcame us. We were alive! We were free.

It was May 5. That evening a Polish woman, the wife of a rabbi, conducted a thanksgiving service. She had found a candle and matches in the sickroom. Some of us prayed. We laughed, we cried. We huddled together until the morning hours. No one was able to sleep.

In the morning the first group of liberators appeared. They were a motley lot of partisans: Poles, Czechs, Hungarians and Yugoslavians. Dirty, bearded, attired in strange garments, they reminded us of a chorus from an itinerant opera company. They were looking for relatives, wives, friends. None were among us. We begged them for food. They shared the only nourishment they carried in their knapsacks: hunks of bacon, called *Paprikaspeck*. The doctor warned us not to eat it. Those who could not resist became deadly sick. A few died. Either the bacon was spoiled or our starved bodies couldn't absorb the fat.

That same afternoon the first detachment of Americans arrived. I wanted to rush up to them and embrace them. I felt an exalted surge of deliverance, but my legs would not carry me. I just smiled and waved.

The Americans looked bewildered. They had heard of concentration camps but they had never seen one. They walked around shaking their heads in disbelief. They had just come from combat, and some of their comrades had been killed that very morning. We were given our first true meal in years: American K-rations. With shaking hands I opened the small, magic package with its incredible treasure: soup cubes, crackers, powdered eggs, Spam, chocolate and a couple of cigarettes. After eating the raw powdered eggs and some of the Spam, I had to give up. I was sick—but happy.

Two days later more Americans arrived—and with them Red Cross nurses and doctors.

We had lived with despair for so long that we only slowly, very slowly, began to understand that we were free.

But before the field kitchen of the Red Cross arrived, Herr Ofenmüller, my foreman at the factory, came looking for me. He shook my hand vigorously. "I am so happy for you, Hanna," he said. "And so is my wife. We hope you will come to our house with me; my wife thought you might want to take a bath."

I could not remember when I had my last bath.

The Ofenmüllers were lower-middle-class Austrians. Their home was clean, the furniture simple and functional. Frau Ofenmüller put her arm around me. The bath was all prepared, a tub filled with steaming hot water. "Just put your clothes in front of the door,"

she said, and handed me a soft large towel and a piece
of soap.

I closed the door. I stepped into the tub—soaking
in the heavenly water until it cooled. The luxury of a
warm bath, the privacy of a room with a closed door,
gave me an indescribable feeling of bliss.

A knock at the door interrupted my reverie. Frau
Ofenmüller told me that she had some clean clothes
for me: they might be a bit too large, but were better
than what I had been wearing.

Like most Austrian women, Frau Ofenmüller was
a fine cook. The food smelled heavenly. A large bowl
of beef broth with juicy pieces of meat and dumplings
was waiting for me. She tried tactfully not to watch
me eat. There was no need to worry. After two spoonsful I ran as fast as I could to the bathroom, where I
became violently ill. Returning to the table I tried
again, but the same thing happened. She had meant
so well, and the soup tasted delicious; I was starved
and yet I could not eat. Embarrassed, I thanked her
and left.

A few days later I went back to the Ofenmüllers
to thank them once more. Frau Ofenmüller had
washed my old clothes in the meantime, but when I
offered to return her dress and shoes, she refused and
insisted I keep them.

As soon as the Red Cross arrived, our camp was
doused with DDT—and so were we. The doctors took
blood samples and gave us injections for whatever
ailed us. Clothing was distributed, as well as tooth-
brushes and soap. The Red Cross field kitchen pro-

vided bland diets for us, and my strength slowly returned. Others were less fortunate. Some inmates died even after the liberation.

The guns were silenced on May 7. The war in Europe was over. Where could we, the survivors, go from here? We were displaced persons, people without a home. Would it still be possible to find any of our loved ones? I knew I would not return to Czechoslovakia.

When a Red Cross official came to the camp to make plans for our repatriation, I decided to go back to Holland. Amsterdam was the only place where I could find out what had happened to Carl. I had survived—why not Carl?

Many of my fellow inmates shared my plight. The Czechs, however, decided to go back to Czechoslovakia. The Germans had quite different feelings, so had the Poles. Most of the Hungarians wanted to return to Hungary; and of course the Dutch had no doubts at all. The population of Holland had behaved remarkably during the years of the German occupation, and many had helped to hide Jews.

We met some of the American soldiers stationed nearby. My English was very poor, but somehow we were able to communicate. We were thrilled and proud to see some Jewish GIs—handsome, tall, sure of themselves, in no way different from their comrades. Our morale had never been higher.

At this time there was no regular train service, no mail, no telephone. Some of the American soldiers who had liberated us had to move on, but before they left, they offered to write to friends or relatives in the States, telling them that we had survived. Prisoners surrounded their jeep as the soldiers entered names and addresses in notebooks. I thought of Walter; maybe he would like to hear that I was alive.

"I have a friend in California," I said in my hesitant school English.

"Where does he live?" the corporal asked.

"Los Angeles." I tried to remember his address. "I think it was Sunset Boulevard."

He laughed. "No number?"

"We'll try," his companion, a sergeant said. He took down my name.

"Walter Kohner," he repeated. "Los Angeles, Sunset Boulevard." He jotted it down and they waved goodbye.

Repatriation started. We began our journey in an army transport plane. My only piece of luggage was a toothbrush sticking out of the pocket of my prison jacket. I had returned Frau Ofenmüller's dress, and again wore the striped jacket with the Star of David and my number affixed to it. We had received some clothing from the Red Cross in the meantime— underwear, a dress and shoes.

Our first stop was a hospital in Ulm, Germany (in the French Zone). During our flight air turbulence made us all sick. Tables loaded with hot chocolate and beautiful open-faced sandwiches were waiting for us at the airport in Ulm. Our stomachs rebelled, and we could not eat. The Red Cross workers looked on disappointedly; they did not understand. At the hospital we were again liberally sprayed with DDT. French doctors examined us, gave us shots and ordered bed rest for a few days.

From Ulm we were transferred to Lindau on the Bodensee, also known as Lake Constance, one of the largest lakes in Europe. On its shores lie Switzerland, Austria and Germany. We stayed in Lindau for a week, in a sanatorium with other ex-prisoners, mostly French, who had arrived previously. An ambulance train took us through Switzerland to Lyons. In Geneva, Swiss women boarded the train and presented each of us with a small package containing a sewing kit, a bar of scented soap—and Swiss chocolate. A red rose came with every package.

Our next stop was Lyons. We underwent another delousing at the local hospital, more shots. In Lyons we slept in a sleazy hotel in the red-light district.

The next day our train trip continued to Brussels. The city, which had been liberated the year before, seemed untouched by the ravages of war. Shops were stuffed with merchandise. People on the street looked well-fed and well-dressed.

Before our departure from Lyons we had received our first ID cards. As DPs (displaced persons), we were entitled to free public transportation and free tickets to any movie house. The Red Cross had given each of us some pocket money, which, for the first time in years, gave us a wonderful sense of freedom.

As in Lyons, our hotel in Brussels was the kind of establishment where you could stay "overnight" any hour of the day. We wondered fleetingly how the venerable Red Cross selected these domiciles for us.

On one of the first afternoons in Brussels, Eva and I decided to go to a movie. We picked *Les Enfants du Paradis*. It was beautiful. But halfway through the film we got fidgety, crouching miserably in our seats. In the darkness we looked at each other. We nodded, and left the ornate old movie theater feeling lost and out of touch with the world.

Depressed, we walked into the late-afternoon sunshine. We stopped at an outdoor café and ordered a café filtre. It was real coffee, bitter and tasty. We lingered over it, watched the crowd around us, and thought about ourselves and what "outsiders" we had become. We wondered whether we would ever again be like ordinary people. It was not the happy afternoon we had planned.

The last stop of our journey was at the Dutch border. A large bus drove us to a nearby monastery, where we joined hundreds of Dutch repatriates. Among them were a number of collaborators who had spent the war years in Germany. These turncoats, too, hoped to be able to go back home, and foolishly expected to escape justice.

My striped prison jacket seemed to confuse the border officials. They separated me from my friends. I had to remain with a group of Dutch Nazis who had been detained in a hall of the monastery waiting to be processed. I watched them tearing up photos, documents and letters. I sat around for hours, not speaking to anybody. Finally I was turned over to a monk who led me out of my last prison. My friends had convinced the Dutch authorities that I was one of them, even though I was the only one who had kept the old jacket with the number and the star and the red stripe on the back.

The monastery seemed idyllic, with rose gardens, vineyards and woods. It was a world by itself, safe and unreal. Still, it was more real to us than Brussels, and I was reluctant to leave.

When we arrived in Amsterdam we were taken to a dormitory near the railroad station. Another bunk, another medical examination. At this point Eva and I separated. She went immediately to Laren, a small town near Amsterdam. Non-Jewish friends there had offered their home for a possible family reunion after the war.

I rushed to the registration center, where lists of Jews who had been deported from Holland and survived concentration camps were fastened with thumbtacks to the office door, with new names being added at least once a day. I saw a few people I had known before the war who were also anxiously looking for survivors. I could find neither Carl's name nor the names of his parents or sister.

It was the end of June, and Amsterdam was still suffering from the shock of the war and the German occupation. Food was scarce, restaurants were closed and the shelves of stores were empty. People looked sad and shabby. When I returned to the dormitory, most of my old friends had gone.

The next morning I went back to the repatriation office. Waiting for another list to arrive, I saw one of Carl's former colleagues who had been with him on the transport from Theresienstadt. He was reluctant to face me—but upon my insistence he finally told me. Carl, on arrival at Auschwitz, had been ordered to the "wrong side." His friend did not know the reason, and I did not ask any questions.

I went back to the dormitory. I tried to rationalize, telling myself that the end had come quickly, that at least he did not have to suffer the horrors and the slow death like so many others. But why? He did not even have a chance. The last time I saw him he had looked relatively healthy and strong; six feet tall, only twenty-six years old. If Carl did not survive, what hope was there for the rest of my family?

I knew now that I was truly alone in the world. Nothing mattered anymore. The euphoria of surviving had gone. A terrifying loneliness overcame me. In this city, which I had once thought of as home, nobody was left to welcome me. No one cared.

Eventually I went to the only place where I thought I might find friends still alive: the house of Coen and Magda. The last time I saw them was in the summer of 1943. While we were in Westerbork they had occasionally sent us food packages; their false papers must have saved them up to that time. But that was two years ago.

Nervously I pressed the doorbell. A maid opened the door. "May I speak to the lady of the house?" I asked.

"She is nursing the baby right now. Would you care to wait?"

So they could not be living here anymore. The baby, I remembered, was about six months old when Carl and I had been deported.

An upstairs door opened and Magda's head peeked

out. She came rushing down the stairs and embraced me. Neither of us had expected to see the other again. I gratefully accepted her invitation to stay at their home.

Magda and Coen had lived there all those years with false ID papers. The house had been one of the meeting places of Amsterdam's underground. Their baby was a new child, born three months before, at the end of the German occupation.

They told me about the few of our friends who had survived. Some had gone into hiding, others had worked in the Resistance.

After dinner, when we sat around the table, Coen asked the inevitable question. The one that I had asked myself over and over again. Why did I survive? Why me?

One of the foremost reasons was luck. If, for instance, Jan had not seen me on my arrival in Auschwitz and had not warned me to hide my pregnancy, I might have revealed it to the SS officer at the selection. If Friedl had not discovered that I was in B Camp, I would certainly have been a victim at the next selection. And so on. Equally important was the help from friends and strangers. No one could have survived without it at one point or another. It started all the way back in Amsterdam with my boss at the Joodse Raad; and in Westerbork with a complete stranger, Walter Hertz, who had befriended Carl and me. He was an old camp inmate who worked in the administration. If he had not taken our names off the list, we would have been on the first transport out of the camp. Why did he do it? Without Eva and some other friends I would never have been able to stand the endless roll calls. If the Russian POW cook had not refused to put rat poison in our food, all of us in Lenzing would have died during the last days. Apart from all the physical help, there was the moral support that many of us gave one another. We could never have done without it.

Maybe it was not a satisfying answer—but it was the best I could give. I will probably live the rest of my life with the question "Why me?" and carry the burden as the price for having been spared.

Walter

"Hier ist Radio Luxembourg, ein Sender der Vereinten Nationen" (This is Radio Luxembourg . . .). I had just finished my noon broadcast. Even though the war in Europe was over, the station's schedule remained the same. News and bulletins focused on the war in the Far East. For one hour every day we broadcast lists of names of foreign workers who had been liberated by Allied forces and were waiting to be repatriated, and names of German POWs. On rare occasions we interviewed high-ranking German officers now prisoners of war.

Robert Breuer stood behind the glass doors of the broadcasting studio and waved at me. It was the day we always had lunch together. As we left, he handed me a letter.

I took a quick look at it. From the familiar return address I could see it came from my brother's office. I was about to open it when Breuer stopped me. "Couldn't that wait? I'm famished."

I stuffed the letter in my pocket. Every Monday we ate at a restaurant called the Rotisserie, a welcome change from the mess hall.

We had just finished the meal when I remembered the letter. I slit open the envelope. It contained another letter, addressed to Walter Kohner, Sunset Boulevard, Los Angeles, California. I studied the unfamiliar handwriting and gave a fleeting thought to the efficiency of the L.A. Post Office in locating an office on twenty-one-mile-long Sunset Boulevard.

A small piece of notepaper fell out. It was dated May 10, 1945. I read:

Dear Sir:
    We are happy to inform you that we have found your friend Hanna Benjamin-Bloch while liberating a concentration camp. She is well and safe.
                                    Cpl. Herbert Shuckart
                                    Sgt. W. Lohmann

I sat still for a moment. Then I read the letter again. I shook my head in disbelief and handed it silently to Breuer. He read it. Finally I found my voice. "What does it mean?" I asked him. "Is she really alive?" He nodded. "Oh my God, I can't believe it," I kept saying. Then I started to laugh, and soon I was shaking with laughter—exultant, jubilant laughter.

Now I studied the letter more carefully. There was an APO number, but it was so badly smudged that it was impossible to decipher. No mention of the location or name of the camp.

How would I find her? Where could she be? Were her parents and her brother still alive, and, above all, her husband?

My first thought was Teplitz. She might have gone back there. I went to see my company commander and showed him the letter. He immediately issued travel orders to Czechoslovakia and a requisition for a jeep. Corporal Dale Pollard from the motor pool was assigned to accompany me. Colonel Rosenbaum, the head of Radio Luxembourg, granted me a leave of absence, furnishing me with a letter of recommendation countersigned by the commanding officer of the Russian section attached to Radio Luxembourg. Czechoslovakia was occupied by Soviet forces and Colonel Rosenbaum believed a formal letter with the hammer-and-sickle stamp would facilitate my passage.

Early next morning Pollard and I were on our way. Within an hour we crossed the German border at Trier. Everywhere we saw devastated towns and villages, blown-up bridges, burned-out vehicles and demolished tanks. Occasionally columns of prisoners, guarded by MPs, passed us.

We detoured around Munich and arrived at ten in the evening at the Russian-Czech demarcation line. Czech and Russian soldiers, guns drawn, stopped us. The Russian colonel's letter granted us swift passage. A few minutes later we were in Czech territory.

The Red Cross station in Karlsbad billeted us at the Hotel Imperial. We received VIP treatment—a bowl of rich potato soup and a slice of dark bread. Czech soldiers accepted our cigarettes and a bar of chocolate.

In the morning I looked for Pollard. His bed was untouched. He turned up at seven, asking me whether I would mind driving alone to my hometown. He had met a nice Czech girl. I wished him well, promising to pick him up within forty-eight hours.

I walked through the town. It was not the Karlsbad I had known. There were no people on the streets and

had some information about Hanna. I talked to an official who had been installed just a few days ago. I offered him a couple of cigarettes. He looked around furtively, making sure that no one was watching, then accepted the gift. To the best of his knowledge, he said, none of the Jews who had lived in Teplitz had returned.

I went to the Bloch's old apartment. I rang the bell. There was no answer. I gazed up at the front of the house and noticed a movement behind the curtains.

It was pouring by now and I decided to find a place to stay overnight. The Hotel Dittrich had been the best hotel in town. It was still there, but the doors were boarded up. I went to the De Saxe, a second-rate hotel before the war, which did have a room. There was no heating. The bed sheets were damp.

A small restaurant was open. I was hungry and walked in. A couple of Czech soldiers were sitting in a corner drinking beer. The air smelled of sweat and stale tobacco. The walls were a dirty green, and sticky. There was nothing to eat but potatoes and sausage. I ate the potatoes but didn't touch the sausage. I had never liked sausage.

I went to my room but didn't undress; I knew I wouldn't sleep. There was one task I had to undertake. Shortly before twelve, I took my canvas bag and went downstairs. The night clerk was asleep. I had to wake him up and ask him to unlock the door. I gave him a chocolate bar from my K-ration. It was still raining. The streets were empty, there were no lights anywhere. I walked directly to my parents' home, only a short distance from the hotel, the house where I had been born and spent my youth. Now the windows were broken and part of the ornate stucco had fallen off the walls.

The garden surrounding the house was gone. Gone too were some of the old fruit trees and the gazebo, a structure of redwood and lattice. I hoped the lush lilac tree in the back of the garden was still there. The lilac tree was the reason for my acting like an intruder on the property that rightfully belonged to me, to my family. It was the spot where my mother had buried the strongbox containing the few pieces of jewelry she had been forced to leave behind.

I looked around cautiously. There was not a sound, except for the heavy raindrops bouncing on the roof. The iron fence encircling the house was gone, and in its place was an ugly wooden enclosure. I scaled it and crossed the garden in search of the lilac tree. It was still there and—miraculously—in full bloom.

Well, I told myself, as I took out a small shovel and a flashlight from my canvas bag, this is certainly like a movie. I began to dig. The rain had softened the ground around the tree. In a few minutes I had piled up a large mound of earth. I heard a sound close by: it was a cat, black and emaciated. The animal watched me as I continued to dig.

My shovel struck something hard. Moments later the strongbox was in my hands. I put it into my canvas bag, filled up the hole and—with a surge of triumph—returned to the hotel. Back in my room, exhausted and soaked and happy, I locked the door and opened the box.

I recognized the few pieces of jewelry my mother wore on festive occasions. They were of no great value. But for her they belonged to a happier past.

The next morning on my way out of Teplitz I visited my father's grave. The gates to the Jewish cemetery were locked. I climbed over the wall and weaved my way through the pathways in the mist. Many of the gravestones lay toppled over and some were missing altogether. Rows of markers were overgrown with crabgrass. I lost my way several times. But then I stood in front of my father's black marble headstone with the inscription:

Here Lies in Peace
Julius Kohner
Born December 12, 1867
Died March 4, 1936
A Blessing to His Family
and The Jewish Nation
Beloved And Unforgotten

I stood there in the rain not quite knowing what to do. I recited the Kaddish and my tears mingled with the raindrops. I picked up a little stone I found nearby, placing it on my father's grave.* Never, I thought, will I return.

On the way back to Karlsbad I crossed the main highway to Prague and decided to take a long detour to the capital. Perhaps Hanna had returned to Prague.

The war had been over four weeks by now, but

---

* According to Jewish lore the stone symbolizes a heavy rock that was placed over the grave in olden times to prevent wild animals from desecrating the remains of the dead.

Prague was still in turmoil. Václavské Náměstí, the city's main artery, was clogged with people. I maneuvered my car through the streets, my American flag fluttering in the wind. People waved at me. I was stopped several times. Girls threw their arms around me and kissed me. I tried to answer some of the frantic questions thrown at me: Where was the mighty American army? Why had General Koniev come to liberate Czechoslovakia and not General Eisenhower? People knew that the American troops had liberated Pilsen—a mere couple of hundred miles from Prague —but why had they stopped there?

I went immediately to the repatriation center, in the old part of the city. There, names of concentration camp survivors who had returned to Czechoslovakia were posted. The few volunteer workers at the center were besieged, husbands looking for wives, mothers for children, children for parents.

The lines were long. An old man with yellow skin searched for the name of the Bloch family. He shrugged regretfully. No one by that name was registered, but if I would like to leave my name and address . . . Crushed, I gave him my APO number and address in Luxembourg.

I had parked my car at the curb. Now I found that it was surrounded by curious gawkers. I forced myself into the driver's seat and blew the horn to clear the way. No one paid any attention, so I blew the horn more urgently and asked them, as gently as I could, to let me go. Then I saw a face that seemed familiar. It belonged to a frail young man with burning eyes— and they were riveted on me. "Walter?" he asked, tentatively.

All I could answer was an equally tentative "Friedl?" and he nodded. I jumped from my car, pushing people away to reach him. We fell into each other's arms. People began to clap their hands. Two brothers or friends or relatives thought dead were holding on to each other in the desperate joy of reunion.

The first thing I said to Friedl was: "Hanna is alive!" He started to cry; he hadn't known. Ever since his return to Prague he had inquired daily at the repatriation office about Hanna. The last time he had been in touch with her was in Auschwitz. He had smuggled himself into the *Waschkolonne* (inmates pushing laundry carts from one compound to the other) trying to see her and get her some warm clothing. When he reached Hanna's compound he found out that she had left on a transport a few hours earlier.

Friedl told me that he and his parents had stayed in Theresienstadt from spring 1943 until December of that year. Then they were all deported to Auschwitz. He had worked as a doctor in the *Familienlager* —the Czech family compound—the only one where entire families were permitted to stay together. In the middle of July 1944 the family compound was liquidated and his parents, together with other elderly inmates, were sent into the gas chambers. Young mothers shared the same fate unless they were willing to separate themselves from their children. Able-bodied men and women were transferred to another compound.

Friedl was transferred to the hospital barracks. On October 28, 1944, the younger inmates of the hospital staff were sent on a transport to the Oranienburg concentration camp near Berlin. There he was one of hundreds of prisoners put to work digging a tunnel. A month later he went to Ohrdruff concentration camp in Thuringia, where he stayed until April 1945. When the Americans came closer he was again put on a transport. U.S. planes, obviously recognizing that the train carried prisoners, bombarded only the railroad tracks. Friedl and other prisoners were forced to walk. Anyone too weak or sick to continue was shot by SS guards and left to die on the road. There was no food or water. The death march lasted for four nights and days. They marched through villages, where people just stared at them, but nobody offered help.

On April 12, 1945, American and Russian artillery came closer. The SS guards changed into Wehrmacht uniforms. The next morning they had disappeared. A small group of Czechs, Friedl among them, got as far as Weimar. A Red Cross truck took them to Prague.

"What happened to Hanna's husband?"

"Probably dead," Friedl said. "I couldn't find a trace of him."

"Poor Hanna," I said.

"Poor Carl."

Then he asked me what I was planning to do. "I will go and look for her in Holland. If Carl's family has survived, they'll be back in Amsterdam." I looked at Friedl's face for a sign of approval.

"It's very likely," Friedl said.

Once more we embraced. I promised to be in touch with him the moment I had any clues of her whereabouts. There was a pause.

"Do you think she'll be glad to see me?"

He smiled. "Very," he said.

I drove back to Karlsbad, returned the car and picked up Pollard. We were lucky to find a ride back to Luxembourg.

My company commander was very understanding. He told me to file a report about the demolished jeep. I thanked him but told him I had to go on trying to find Hanna. Again he was most helpful, and cutting all red tape, he dispatched me on a "Mission to Holland." "But this time," he added, "bring back the jeep."

I left early the following day and arrived in the afternoon in Naarden-Bussum. My first stop was City Hall. A friendly young man showed me the list of people who had returned since the end of the war. Hanna's name was not on the list, nor were those of her relatives. He suggested I leave my name and APO number. Then he gave me the address of the Amsterdam repatriation center. Around noon the next day I drove into Amsterdam.

It was a fine summer day. Banners stretched from house to house proclaiming a festival of liberation. Dutch flags fluttered everywhere. As I headed toward the former Jewish ghetto, where the repatriation center was located, I scanned the sidewalks tensely, fixing my eyes on every woman walking alone, in the foolish and desperate hope of recognizing Hanna.

At the repatriation office, an old building in the Joodenbuurt, I waited my turn. There were about fifty people in line.

"I am looking for a friend of mine by the name of

Bloch," I told the man behind a desk. "She also might be listed under Benjamin. That was her married name. Hanna Benjamin." My voice was trembling slightly.

He reached for a file with the letter *B*, let his fingers run along long rows of names, and shook his head.

"Sorry. But maybe if you want to leave your name . . ."

"Thanks," I murmured, and jotted down my name and APO number.

I was walking down the dark corridor toward the exit when I heard a frantic voice calling, "Sergeant Kohner!"

The official came running after me. "Just wait a moment. There is a file with new returnees, which I haven't looked through. Yesterday someone else was on duty. Come along." And he led me back to his office.

I felt numb but I noticed that the man's hands were also trembling as he opened a file and leafed through a bunch of notes and letters.

"Here it is," he said, triumphantly. "Hanna Benjamin, née Bloch, is staying with Dr. Van Emde Boas. I'll write down the address. It's not too far from here. Amsterdam-Zuid."

I practically tore the note from his hand and ran out of the room. At the end of the corridor I realized that I hadn't even thanked him.

Once more I ran back, reached out and shook his hand. "Thank you," I said, "thank you. *Dank u wel.*" It was one of the few Dutch phrases I knew.

A number of times I had to ask for directions to Amsterdam-Zuid. Stadionweg 80 was a two-story villa surrounded by a garden. I stopped for a moment. My heart skipped a beat. I rang the bell. After a few seconds the door was opened by a maid.

"I'd like to see Hanna," I said.

"Please come in."

"How is she? I haven't seen her for seven years . . . is she all right?"

The girl smiled. "She is fine. Who should I say . . . ?"

"Don't say a thing. This is a surprise. Please—just tell her someone is here to see her. Don't mention the uniform, please, will you?"

She smiled, nodded and ran up the stairway.

My body tensed. I listened. I had waited for this moment for so long.

There were muffled voices upstairs. Then steps. I looked up.

Halfway down the stairs, she stopped. She stared at me, and then—stretching out her arms—she flew toward me.

Epilogue

Walter and Hanna were married in Luxembourg on October 24, 1945. They moved to Los Angeles in July 1946.

After a number of miscarriages due to the abortion in Auschwitz, Hanna gave birth to a daughter, Julie, on July 4, 1955.

Walter is an artist's representative in Hollywood.

In May 1953 Ralph Edwards, producer and host of the *This Is Your Life* show, televised Hanna's life story. A number of people who played an important role in Hanna's life appeared as surprise guests on the show. Among them Corporal Shuckart, one of the GI's who liberated Hanna's camp and wrote the letter to Walter. The climax of the evening was the reunion with her brother Friedl, who was living in Israel and whom she hadn't seen for fifteen years. In 1956 Friedl and his family emigrated to the United States. He is a psychiatrist now living in Los Angeles.

Hanna's parents, Max and Hertha Bloch, were killed in Auschwitz in July 1944.

Carl Benjamin was killed in Auschwitz, October 1944.

Irene Benjamin returned to Amsterdam.

Dr. Max Benjamin survived and returned to Amsterdam; his wife, Irma Benjamin, died in Bergen-Belsen in 1945.

Uncle Sigmund and Aunt Rosie were killed in Auschwitz.

Grandmother Birnbaum died in Theresienstadt in December 1943.

Cousin Martha and her husband were killed in Auschwitz; their children were hidden throughout the Occupation by various Dutch families. They still live in Holland.

Walter's mother, Helene Kohner, died in Los Angeles, December 1952.

Eva lives in Long Beach, California; she is married and has two daughters.

Franz Ofenmüller of Lenzing, Austria, died in 1960.

Dr. Coen Van Emde Boas died in Amsterdam, 1981; his wife, Magda, survives him.

Alice lives in Liechtenstein; she has two children.

Lilo and husband Michael both died in Auschwitz.

Sergeant Robert Breuer lives in New York, where he is married and has two daughters.

Richard Tauber went to London, where he successfully continued his career as a singer as well as a conductor. He died in 1948.

SS Commandant Gemmeke of Camp Westerbork, is supposed to be still living in Düsseldorf, Germany.